Anglican and Evangelical?

RICHARD TURNBULL

continuum

Continuum International Publishing Group
The Tower Building, 11 York Road, London SE1 7NX
80 Maiden Lane, Suite 704, New York NY 10038

www.continuumbooks.com

First published 2007

British Library Cataloguing-in-Publication Data
A catalogue record for this book is available from the British Library.

ISBN: 0–8264–8164–7 (paperback)

Typeset by Kenneth Burnley, Wirral, Cheshire
Printed and bound in Great Britain by MPG Books Ltd, Bodmin, Cornwall

Contents

This book is dedicated to my family.

To Caroline, my beloved wife,
who has supported me throughout.

To my children, Sarah, Katie, Matt and Rebecca,
who will enjoy seeing their names in print.

Abbreviations

BCMS	Bible Churchmen's Missionary Society
Bible Society	British and Foreign Bible Society
CMS	Church Missionary Society
CPAS	Church Pastoral Aid Society
CSU	Church Socialist League
ECUSA	Episcopal Church of the USA
LCM	London City Mission
SPG	Society for the Propagation of the Gospel

Introduction

What does it mean to be both Anglican and Evangelical? A passion for the Bible, for truth and for a spiritually deep relationship with Jesus Christ characterizes both of these Christian traditions. Evangelicalism and Anglicanism often, perhaps increasingly, combine in the same person. As Principal of an Anglican Evangelical theological college, and Tutor in Church History and Anglicanism, I find many students coming to train for the ministry for whom the historic basis of both traditions and their relationship is shrouded in mystery. Not all Evangelicals are Anglican and not all Anglicans are Evangelical. However, in terms of significant churches, leaders both ordained and lay, finance and influence, and candidates for ordination, Anglican Evangelicalism is an important movement.

Thus it is both important and necessary for Evangelicals to understand and appreciate their own tradition (why are some more Reformed and others more charismatic?). Equally significant is insight into how Evangelicalism relates to Anglicanism. Increased awareness of what it means to be an Anglican Evangelical can only be beneficial to future ministers, lay leadership and many in other Anglican traditions who also want deeper understanding. Indeed, one of the objectives of this book is to enhance understanding of the whole range of traditions within Anglicanism and how they have developed.

Why does tension arise within the Anglican Church between Evangelicals and others? What are the flashpoints and underlying theological issues? These questions too will be explored. Hard questions will not be avoided. We will need to ask whether there is a core Anglican identity and what belongs to it, as well as what belongs to the periphery. Not all the conclusions will be palatable to everyone. Partly this is because much of the public presentation of Anglicanism today so often represents only one particular stream of Anglican development; and may, indeed, not represent the historic core of the tradition.

Another key objective of this book is to draw back the veil which has come to shroud the historic Anglican tradition and to re-establish the roots of the modern Anglican Evangelical. In doing so, I pray that mutual dialogue, appreciation and illumination within Anglicanism may increase, even if some may differ in their conclusions. Genuine conversation must start from acceptance, respect and understanding. In times when there are serious questions concerning the identity of Anglicanism, amid danger of fracture, this book is a particular contribution to understanding the Evangelical tradition within and beyond the bounds of the Anglican Church.

There are a few technical points to note. Much ink is expended over whether Evangelical or Anglican is the adjective; is it Anglican Evangelical or Evangelical Anglican? There is some danger that this can lead to largely sterile and unfruitful debate. Throughout this book the terminology will be Anglican Evangelical, but too much should not be read into it. Evangelicalism is not just a movement within various denominations (although, of course, it is that). It is also a way of understanding the faith. As such it has a prior claim to any denominational allegiance, however closely related they may be. Hence, in this text the noun is Evangelical and the adjective is Anglican; hence Anglican Evangelical. More importantly, the two are seen as belonging together in significant ways; and that is of greater import than the order.[1]

Evangelicals argue about all sorts of things. So do the scholars of Evangelicalism. Should Evangelical be capitalized? Once again, the conclusion may not matter enormously, but throughout the text Evangelical as a noun is capitalized (unless explicitly demanded by the context). One further point concerns the use of the term 'Anglican'. The origin lies in the nineteenth century and so it is in some ways anachronistic to use the terminology to describe the post-Reformation English Church before then. It is, however, enormously convenient to do so. Hence 'Anglicanism' will be freely used in this book in that way, but it must be borne in mind that this is for descriptive convenience rather than contemporary accuracy. In general terms the use of 'Anglican' will be for when discussing matters of wider application and 'Church of England' for issues relating specifically to the English Church and context; though the distinction is not always a straightforward one.

Many thanks are due, most importantly to my family. My wife, Caroline, has shouldered the burden of her husband writing a book in the first year of a new job! She has done so with characteristic fortitude, good humour and understanding, not least when the burden was greatest. My children also, Sarah, Katie, Matthew and Rebecca, who have endured a move of house and school. I should like to thank Carolyn Armitage, my commissioning editor, who encouraged me with much understanding and generosity during the writing. Finally, I thank the students and staff of Wycliffe Hall. The students, on whom I tested out numerous aspects of my thinking on Anglicanism, and from whom I learned a great deal in discussion. The staff, who have not only had to get used to a new principal, but who have been generous, understanding and interested in this writing project.

Richard Turnbull
Oxford, Summer 2006

Notes

1   See the helpful discussion in R. T. France and A. E. McGrath (eds) (1993), *Evangelical Anglicans*, London, SPCK, pp. 1–20.

1

Understanding Anglican identity

The quest for identity

Identifying the issues

What does it mean to be Anglican?

Walk into an Anglican church in England. You might find anything from a High Mass, with numerous robed assistants in the sanctuary, to an informal youth service with guitars and drums. The focal point might be the sacrament, the sermon or the music. It might be a country parish with 20 people meeting in a medieval church to ecumenical experimentation in an area of new housing. The sermon might last five minutes or 40, and vary from scriptural exposition to reflections on current events. Holy Communion (which might also be called the Eucharist, the Lord's Supper or the Mass) might involve bread or wafers, together with a variety of dress, liturgical emphasis, choreography and symbolism. An organ, an orchestra, a small music group, choir or a band may lead the music. The worship may be reserved or exuberant. The description could go on.

Walk into an Anglican church in the USA. You will find more uniformity on the surface. Careful observation, however, will also reveal a good deal of variation. In some places Eucharist, in others Morning Prayer and, occasionally, the beginnings of more informal approaches to worship, though probably greater liturgical uniformity. The teaching and its content are likely to be prominent and to mark out the particular stance of the church as more or less orthodox. The more conservative will use the 1928 Book of Common Prayer rather than the more radical revision of 1979. At least some ceremonial aspects of worship and ministry may feature more prominently.

Walk into an Anglican church in Africa. Some of the greatest contrasts will be seen. The church may meet outdoors. Traditional clerical dress is likely to be in evidence alongside drums, music, dancing and a more flexible approach to timekeeping. The teaching will be firmly based upon biblical exposition with explicit commitment to commonly accepted Christian teaching. Clergy may be more thinly spread, travel many miles and be largely self-supporting through farming or other employment. The challenges of poverty and AIDS will be all around.

What is the link that merits the description Anglican?

Approaches to definition

A variety of alternatives may be used to define Anglican. A *theological* definition of Anglicanism is the assertion of a common doctrinal core and belief to Anglicanism. This claim is prior to any discussion of the substance of that doctrinal identity. Rather it is about a method of approach. It is, however, a claim that belief is more central than form or style of expression. Identity here is essentially *confessional*, based around an accepted and historic understanding of Christian faith. For some the core consists of the agreed truth in the Bible and perhaps reflected in the Creeds. For others a particular aspect of Anglican theological history or development might be given the most weight.

A *sociological* definition of Anglicanism is a statement that belonging to a common family is the essence of what unites Anglicans. It is a popular hypothesis of sociologists of religion, and some other commentators, that belonging comes before believing.[1] This may be expressed globally that belonging to the international family of Anglican Churches is the key defining characteristic of Anglicanism. Form and family are emphasized over content and confession. Similarly, in respect of the Church of England, church leaders frequently note the 2001 census result of 72 per cent of the population claiming to be Christian[2] (when perhaps 10 per cent attend worship on a regular basis). Significant clergy time and church attention are directed towards the sociological definitions of church as expressed through the 'occasional offices', baptism, marriage and funerals. Emphasis is given to the communal aspects of church, ministry to the whole community rather than pastoring the flock of the committed. These are all expressions of a sociological definition of the Church and of Anglicanism.

An *experiential* definition is one that primarily reflects the claim that Anglicanism is united by common prayer. In whatever part of the nation or the world, the Anglican worshipper will experience sufficient customary elements to be recognizably Anglican. These may include doctrinal aspects of belief, but expressed in the worship and liturgy, for example, the Creed or the Lord's Prayer. Even in an age of liturgical experimentation, the framework will reflect a common understanding of common prayer.

Alternatively, perhaps there is a simple structural framework for Anglicanism in its organization and governance? Many people, from a wide variety of church traditions, hold, in practice, a *structural* or *legal* view of the Church. The intellectual approach to understanding the Church in this way gives emphasis to the role and place of the episcopate in Anglican polity (that is, the form of organization, constitution and government) and in the structure and development of canon law and synodical government. However, it also has a popular expression. Clergy may view the Anglican Church as the body which ordains them, pays them and provides a pension or housing. More widely, this is the organization upon whose councils and synods people sit, which baptizes, marries and buries, exacts financial assessments and provides bishops and other officials. This is more the Church of 'the diocese' rather than 'the parish'. It is an essentially organizational view of the Church. It has adherents at every level of both Church and civic government.

Anglican identity reflects elements of each of these four methodological approaches. Simply an appreciation of that fact helps in understanding the variety of Anglican expression. No one approach can fully explain the nuances and complexities of Anglicanism. However, it is pertinent to ask whether there is a central kernel of definition, around which other elements ebb and flow. What belongs to the essence of identity and what other aspects are added in order to build the diverse and varied impression of modern Anglicanism?

Essential to understanding the trajectory of this book is the critical centrality of a theological definition and understanding of Anglicanism while also seeking to understand the nature of that core and the diversity around it.

Reaching back: pre-Reformation snapshots of the Church

Beginnings

When did the Church of England begin? The question is important in establishing identity. The central point is the nature of continuity and discontinuity in the historical development of Anglicanism. For a historian such analysis is part of the tools of the trade. To what extent is there a seamless whole or are particular events, movements or periods discontinuous with the overall direction of the Anglican story? To those who emphasize the catholicity of the Church (that is, the universal oneness of the Church in continuity with the first five centuries of Christianity), certain periods loom larger in the discussion: the pre-Reformation period, the Caroline Divines of the seventeenth century and, for some, the Catholic renewal of the nineteenth century. For others, providential history (the sovereignty of God over history) is expressed in the Reformation and Evangelical Revival. The decisions made have implications for identity. It is not so much of 'right and wrong' answers, but of understanding the differing approaches.

It has generally been those who give most weight to the Catholic continuity of the Church who have most eagerly reached back into the pre-Reformation picture of the Church. It is manifestly the case that there is a story of the Church in England prior to the Reformation – the *ecclesia anglicana* (the English Church). The reality, however, is somewhat more complex than the myth. Rarely is this sort of debate unpacked further. A snapshot of the English Church prior to the Reformation reveals a complexity and diversity substantially at variance with rather simplistic assertions of continuity. Considering the Church in England between AD 500 and AD 1500, which pictures will be drawn? The choice is varied and instructive. The arrival of Augustine of Canterbury's mission from Pope Gregory or the spread of Celtic Christian influence from Iona and the north-east of England? The monastic movement, its development and renewal, or the Lollards and the first introduction of the Bible (at least in part) in English? Identity depends on which pictures are emphasized and drawn upon. An informed understanding of Anglican identity requires recognition of this variety.

Two pictures can illustrate by way of example.

The mission of Augustine of Canterbury

The first of these pictures is to look back to the very first stirrings of Christianity in England, its form and identity. We know very little about the earliest appearances of Christianity in these lands, apart from a scattering of references amongst early writers such as Tertullian, Origen and Hippolytus. Among individuals we know of Alban, the martyr, and Pelagius, the heretic, against whom St Augustine of Hippo defended orthodoxy. In AD 597 Pope Gregory sent the monk, Augustine, on a mission to England. The rationale behind the enterprise was to convert the heathen of England, its tribes and kings. That mission was remarkably successful; and as we know, history is often written by the victors. Augustine landed in Kent, with 40 companions. We know of the encounter with the English king of the region from Bede.[3] The English king was Ethelbert, whose wife, Bertha, was a Christian. For the first few days he kept the missionaries at bay, before agreeing to hear them in the open air. Within a few weeks Ethelbert was converted and subsequently other kings were also converted to the faith, though politics was at least a significant partner to faith – a historic tension throughout Anglican history. As the kings were converted, so were the people; that was the deal. The question of how deep the conversion went is, of course, an open one. However, we see here the conversion of England from the top; the king followed by the people. The king would inevitably be attracted by the Roman model of order and authority.

We need to note four things. First, that the king's wife was already a Christian. In other words the mission of Augustine was not the first entry into England of Christian witness. Second, that the conversion of the king led to the conversion of the people, already a national and institutional approach to the Church taking shape. Third, that there was at the same time an alternative strand of Christianity affecting England, from the Celts. Fourth, the main source, Bede, though a responsible historian, was writing from the point of view of Roman Christianity which was the outlook that prevailed.

The Celtic strand of Christianity

The Celts represented a quite different strand of Christianity. If the Roman model was institutional, ordered and organized, the Celtic was charismatic, flexible and ad hoc. The Celtic influence originated in the foundation of the Abbey of Iona by missionaries from Ireland. Key figures were Ninian and Patrick, and in AD 563 Columba left Ireland with 12 companions and landed at Iona. He built a monastery and laboured there for the next 30 years, dying in AD 597, the same year as Pope Gregory launched his mission to England. A Northumbrian prince, Oswald, became a Christian while in exile on Iona, returning to Northumberland as king in AD 633 and asking Iona to send a missionary. So it was that from Iona monk missionaries set out for the north-east of England, Cuthbert and Aidan in particular. They established a monastery on Lindisfarne, Iona in Northumberland, and their influence spread as far south as York.

There are two particular points of interest for us in the story. First, what was common and what was different between the Celtic and Roman forms of Christianity and, second, the ultimate triumph of the Roman model. It is important not to elevate, exaggerate or even to baptize the Celtic model in contrast to the Roman. Both were episcopal. They built an understanding of the Church around a consecrated, ordained leader as bishop. So, while Augustine became the first Archbishop of Canterbury, Cuthbert was also ordained bishop. Both models were missionary in orientation. There was a shared explicit desire to convert the heathen. The points of contrast are more to do with the manner of execution. The Roman model was both territorial and institutional. The concern was with the conversion of nations, perhaps led by the king, from the 'top down'. There was the immediate issue of compromise when Christianity became, once again, so closely connected institutionally with the civic authorities. The Celtic model was more charismatic in essence. Bishops were not ordained to territories, but expressly to bring the mission of Jesus directly to the ordinary people. The Celtic saints sought a closeness expressed in resistance to Roman pomp and circumstance. They walked rather than rode on horseback, they emphasized the prophetic and the miraculous and an incarnational closeness to nature. Hence there was less need of an organized, institutional framework or polity, greater freedom and more flexibility. It was

the institutional failure of the Celtic model to organize that contributed to its defeat, embodied in the decision of the Synod of
Whitby regarding the date of Easter – a classic example of a minor
matter reflecting a significantly greater issue of principle.

There were of course many weaknesses in the Celtic model as
well as strengths in the Roman. David Edwards has drawn attention to them with a rather sweeping assertion, which illustrates
both the victory and the continuing dominance within Anglicanism of the Roman model:

> But for all the attractiveness of the humble and holy men asso-
> ciated with Lindisfarne, they lacked something: authority to
> teach a creed, to organize an institution, to command.[4]

The Church of England (and Anglicanism more widely) especially, but not only, in its more Catholic understanding, reflects
the triumph of the Roman model in its ecclesiological and leadership patterns very deeply indeed. The key point is that England
experienced two authentic expressions of the Christian faith in
these early years. Hence when the question of continuity is raised,
the question is: of continuity with what? The answer to that
question affects all sorts of aspects of identity and definition.

John Wyclif and the Lollards

John Wyclif[5] is a towering figure in pre-Reformation England. In
both his theological concerns and his practical expression we see
a radicalism which laid very significant foundations indeed for the
Reformation. Into the ferment of medieval England, as writers
argue over the extent of the nature of medieval piety (the mystical
writings of Thomas à Kempis, Walter Hilton, Richard Rolle and
the author of the *Cloud of Unknowing*, vying in scholarly debate
with cults, indulgences, purgatory and transubstantiation as the
authentic view of medieval Christianity), enter the first English
Protestants, though it is anachronistic to refer to them as such.[6]

John Wyclif

John Wyclif was born around 1330 and was an Oxford don up to
around 1378. If the description of John Foxe in his 'Book of

Martyrs'[7] of Wyclif being the 'Morning Star of the Reformation' is polemical, then so is the assertion of his latest biographer, Gillian Evans, that 'it is far from certain that Wyclif translated a single word of the Bible into English'.[8] Wyclif remains a central figure in the history of the English Church, of Protestantism and of Bible translation.

Wyclif was trained in the classic disciplines of medieval Oxford before becoming a Doctor of Theology. He increasingly attacked clerical wealth and corruption, not least amongst the itinerant friars. This was, in itself, not especially likely to bring him unwelcome attention from the authorities except that Wyclif began to analyse the theological consequences of his critique of the Church. He lectured upon the Church, the papacy, the Bible and the Eucharist. He criticized the way in which the poor were unable to gain the benefits of the system of indulgences. He also wrote about the relationship of the secular state and the Church (and did not endear himself to the papacy with his views on papal taxation).

In 1377 papal Bulls were issued against Wyclif intended to provoke action by both the king and the University. It was Wyclif's teaching on the nature of the Church and authority of the papacy that attracted most attention. Conveniently, first the king (Edward III) and, a year later, the Pope (Gregory X1), died. The Archbishop's panel examining the papal Bulls ordered Wyclif to cease his teaching in these areas. In Oxford the examination concentrated on his eucharistic theology and he was condemned by a committee under the Chancellor, William Barton, who had long disputed with Wyclif. Evans points out that Wyclif himself asserted that his views in denial of transubstantiation derived from after his removal from Oxford.[9] Withdrawing to his parish of Lutterworth, Wyclif, protected by powerful and influential lay patrons, continued to write and publish polemical pamphlets. This was not a fully worked-out Reformation (not least the absence in explicit terms of the idea of justification by faith). However, essential to his theological standpoint was the critique of corruption, transubstantiation, the role of the papacy, the centrality of the Bible, the supremacy of Christ and the predestination of the elect. The Bible, he argued, should be in the hands of the people in a language which they understood.

It was inevitable that alongside Wyclif's passion for the Church to be reclaimed for the people, not least the poor, and with his views on ministry, that he would be drawn to the issue of language as the means of communication. English was beginning to develop as a language for business, although Latin remained the tongue of the Church. Translations of the Bible are rarely the product of one person. Hence the description, 'Wyclif's Bible', reflects the source of the inspiration and direction as much as the detailed work. The translation of the Scriptures into English took place between about 1380 and 1396 and involved a team of scholars, working from the Latin Vulgate translation. It is inconceivable that Wyclif was not involved in some way and it was he who certainly provided the theological framework and coherence into which this important early work was written. Gillian Evans points out the difficulty of separating myth from reality in the history of Wyclif.[10] Nevertheless, whatever flowed from Wyclif's pen, his significance was foundational to the beginnings of the Reformation in England. Indeed, his ideas also spread on the continent of Europe through John Hus, whose opinions were remarkably similar to those of Wyclif.

The Lollards

After Wyclif's death his supporters continued to propagate his ideas. The role of the laity in the spread of Reformation principles is significant in both the history of the Reformation and more broadly in the history of ideas. It is difficult to deny that Wyclif and his later followers, the Lollards (though it was an adherence claimed by the Lollards rather than by Wyclif himself), prepared the ground for the later claims of the Reformation. By 1395, just a few years after the death of Wyclif in 1384, there was an active group of Lollard partisans in Parliament. The Lollards – the origin of the name is shrouded in mystery but probably means 'mumblers' – were mainly common people, some artisans and merchants and a few aristocratic sympathizers. Oppression gradually reduced Lollard influence but on the eve of the Reformation at the end of the fifteenth century there were significant groups in the Chilterns, in Essex and in London. There are numerous examples of charges against Lollards; denying transubstantiation and purgatory and reading the Scriptures in English were the most common. There were a number of burnings of those who failed to recant. Lollard groups provided ready-made points of reception for the smuggling of New Testaments, not least Tyndale's translation, and there were strong links to the merchants of the woollen trade.

The theological and spiritual importance of the Lollards can be seen from the Twelve Conclusions, published in 1395, which covered a range of matters from the state of the Church, the priesthood and transubstantiation to prayers for the dead, confession, war and other matters. The first principle which they advocated was that of reform:

> We poor men, treasures of Christ and his Apostles, denounce to the Lords and Commons of the Parliament certain conclusions and truth for the reformation of the Holy Church of England . . .[11]

The papacy and the whole industry of medieval piety came under scrutiny. The claim to authority was located in Scripture, there was a radical note in resistance to arms and an early intellectual claim to the Reformation call of *ad fontes*, the return to original sources and to antiquity:

> We pray God of his endless goodness reform our Church, all out of joint, to the perfections of the first beginning. Amen.[12]

So, whatever the complexities, there was a popular Protestantism prior to the Reformation and the early stirrings of the demand for reform. The complete portrait of Anglican understanding demands the fullness of the picture of pre-Reformation England, some elements of which have become obscured.

Reformed or Catholic: was there a Reformation?

The focus of the debate on continuity and discontinuity in the Anglican tradition is centred on the place of the Reformation. It is returning to the question: when did the Church of England begin? There is an extensive debate over the nature and place of the Reformation in England and its role in the origins of the Church of England. The greater the emphasis placed upon Catholic continuity within the Church of England, the lesser is the role given to the Reformation. This has been illustrated most particularly by the influence of the Oxford Movement upon Anglican history and self-understanding. We will look in more detail at this movement subsequently. For the moment suffice it to say that, ultimately, the Reformation was not to be allowed to stand in the way of the Oxford Movement's claim to catholicity.

Church and state

The understanding of the English Reformation is closely connected to the whole area of the relationship of the Church and the state. Indeed, this relationship is remarkably important in both Protestant and English religious history, as we have already observed in embryonic form in the conversion of the first English kings. We see it also in the wider Reformation expressed, in different ways, through Luther's[13] notion of the 'godly prince' and Calvin's[14] development of the 'godly city' of Geneva – both examples of the Magisterial Reformation; that is, Reformation achieved through civic order and the civil magistrate.

A particular version of this occurred in England. Henry VIII loved theology and was under no illusion that he had been placed upon the English throne through God's providence. Henry read Luther and did not like what he read. His title 'Defender of the Faith' was awarded by the Pope in 1521 as a reward for putting his name to a document against Luther. It was Henry's personal life which began to cause problems. Henry married his deceased brother's widow, Catherine of Aragon. No male heir was produced. Henry argued that in the eyes of God the marriage had not been a legitimate one. The Pope disagreed. An added ingredient was the attractions of Anne Boleyn, whose family were significant supporters of the Reformation. Henry asserted himself against the Pope by relying upon the idea of the king as the Supreme Head of the Church. This particular defence of the 'King's Great Matter' was worked up by his team of advisers including the Cambridge don, Thomas Cranmer. Acts of Parliament were steered through between 1533 and 1536 to secure Henry's position by his chief officer of state, Thomas Cromwell, another reformer. Cranmer became Archbishop of Canterbury in 1532[15] and with Cromwell moved against the images of popular Catholicism such as shrines and church furnishings. Concurrently, the state moved against monastic foundations and their lands. This period represents an intricate interplay of reformers and conservatives in the administration, juggling between Henry's vacillating religious opinions and his political ambitions. Cromwell fell from power in 1540 and was executed on trumped-up charges of heresy; some supporters of the Reformation were burnt as well as Catholic opponents, and at times Cranmer's own position seemed precarious. In 1536 the English exile, William Tyndale, responsible for the first English translation of the New Testament, was martyred at the hands of the continental authorities in Belgium after being betrayed. Tyndale was translating directly from the original languages, using the Greek New Testament, published by Erasmus in 1516, unlike Wyclif's early manuscript version which was based on the Latin Vulgate version from around AD 390. Tyndale's New Testament had been flooding into England, at first in the hands of the later Lollards. In 1536–37 Henry ordered the provision of English Bibles in every parish church and sponsored an official translation in 1539. Although there was some backtracking in 1543 the direction was becoming clearer.

The Protestant paradise

Henry's complicated and ambiguous Reformation was swept away with the accession of Edward VI in 1547. Opportunity beckoned. Cranmer's mature eucharistic theology was continuing to develop in a Reformed direction, though Henry himself never departed from his understanding of the real presence. Two prayer books were produced in Edward's reign. The 1549 version was a first move, radical in a number of ways, building on an earlier translation of the Communion rite into English in 1548. Few really liked it. For Protestants there was frustration at the pace of change. Cranmer's caution, however, was well advised with a Catholic uprising in 1549. In 1552 a significant and clearly Protestant prayer book was produced. Similarly, Cranmer produced a statement of doctrine and a draft of canon law revision. The Protestant Reformation was marching on. Then disaster struck. The king died. The rightful heir was Mary Tudor, Henry's daughter by Catherine of Aragon. The Protestant establishment was thrown into chaos. The Duke of Northumberland, Edward's chief minister, moved to establish Lady Jane Grey, a Protestant minor member of the royal family, on the throne, but he failed to restrain Mary, who rode out from London and raised an army. Within two weeks the crown was in the hands of Mary Tudor; both Jane and Northumberland were executed. Protestants were fleeing in exile to the continent and Cranmer and the Protestant bishops had little hope.

Bloody Mary

So began the reign of Bloody Mary, with hundreds of Protestants burnt at the stake. These included Bishops Hooper, Ridley, Latimer and Archbishop Cranmer himself, but also merchants, tradesmen and ordinary men and women released through the Protestant faith from the turmoil of purgatory, indulgences and salvation by works. Mercifully, in the grace of God, Mary's reign was just five years long and she was succeeded by the Protestant daughter (Princess Elizabeth) of the Protestant Queen (Anne Boleyn).

Formative role of the Reformation

The life and death of Archbishop Cranmer is of far-reaching significance in the formation of Anglicanism and its self-understanding. The doctrinal bases of his liturgical reform and the groundwork that led to the Thirty-Nine Articles are essential to Anglicanism. The martyrdoms in Mary's reign are also of foundational importance for the identity of Anglican Evangelicals.

It is difficult to deny the formative role of the Reformation on the polity, theology and ministry of the Church of England. While some scholars seek to emphasize the pre-Reformation *ecclesia anglicana*, the traditional doyen of Anglican studies, Stephen Sykes, firmly places the commencement of the ecclesial life of the Church of England within the context of the Reformation.[16] Similarly, Diarmaid MacCulloch, author of a magisterial work on Thomas Cranmer, reminds us that the reign of Edward VI – that most Protestant of monarchs in that most Protestant of times – decisively and permanently shaped the identity of Anglicanism.[17] Roman Catholic scholars, such as Eamon Duffy, although giving weight to the continued existence of popular Catholic piety, also note the centrality of the Reformation for Anglicanism, albeit a Reformation from above. This message and analysis is often unpopular among contemporary Anglicans, many of whom have a historic understanding of Anglicanism formed and shaped by the Catholic renewal of the nineteenth century, but which bears little resemblance to the reality at the time.

Digging the foundations: doctrinal building blocks

The Book of Common Prayer, the Thirty-Nine Articles of Religion and the Ordinal together form the *formularies* of the Church of England. In other words they are the foundation stones and building blocks upon which the Church of England as an institution was built. Their content and provenance then is of the utmost importance for Anglicans generally and Anglican Evangelicals in particular. These documents have become obscured in the life of the Church, in preparation for ministry and in general awareness among both worshippers and decision-makers. E. J. Bicknell's major theological treatment of the Articles is dated, dry and obscure, affected by the author's liberal Catholic presuppositions.[18] Thus a veil is being gradually drawn over the Protestant heritage of Anglicanism, which needs to be drawn back. This shrouding of the heritage is most prominent in the Episcopal Church of the USA (ECUSA); indeed even the recognition that the constitutional name of that Church is the *Protestant* Episcopal Church of the USA illustrates the point. A similar point could be made in respect of the history of subscription (i.e. an oath of adherence) to the Thirty-Nine Articles in the Church of England, ended in 1975.

The Prayer Books

Although most people within the life of the Church are aware of the Book of Common Prayer of 1662, fewer are conscious either of the antecedents to that Prayer Book or its doctrinal importance. The development of the Prayer Book in the 1550s was a crucial aspect of the development, both doctrinal and liturgical, of Anglicanism. The nature of Anglicanism can only be understood by gaining insight and understanding into this process. It has rarely been exposed to public exposition in accessible form.

Few could have realized the impact that the appointment of Thomas Cranmer as Archbishop would have upon the history of

England and of Anglicanism. MacCulloch details the full dramatic and scholarly description of Cranmer's life and career.[19] Brief comment will suffice here. Although the religious convictions of Henry VIII remain for the scholar somewhat shrouded, those of his Archbishop do not. During the 1530s and 1540s Cranmer was moving inexorably in a more Protestant direction in both his personal convictions and in public policy. That is neither to disguise the fact that such movement was not neat and linear, nor to fail to recognize that there was compromise, political intrigue and posturing along the way. Indeed, Cranmer's survival from 1534 to 1558 is itself a remarkable testimony to his political prowess. Cranmer's convictions, not least in respect of his theological understanding of the Holy Communion, were moving away not only from the traditional Catholic understanding of *transubstantiation*, but also away from the Lutheran notion of *real presence*, to a much more Reformed understanding of the presence of Christ, which became known as *receptionism*, a position, in fact, closer to Zwingli[20] than to Calvin.

There were three Prayer Books in the period 1548 to 1560, two authored by Cranmer himself, in 1549 and 1552, and one, in 1559, in the early days of the reign of Elizabeth. In 1548 Cranmer published his *Order for Holy Communion*, in essence a translation of the canon of the Mass into English. This was a precursor to the publication of the Prayer Book of 1549. It is very important to understand the depth of the changes made in these Prayer Books. The details are set out in the excursus on page 19. In outline, we see a number of trends. First, the adoption of the vernacular. The 1549 Prayer Book, building upon the 1548 *Order*, was the first major liturgical book to be published in English. This principle was maintained in all subsequent revisions. The significance for the cause of the Reformation should not be underestimated. The vernacular in general and English in particular was the language of reform. This trend was reinforced by Cranmer's production of the Book of Homilies. The Bible was to be preached in English, even if the clergy themselves were not capable of preparation and spiritual insight.

Second, the trend of Protestant doctrine in the development of Anglican liturgy is unmistakable and of huge importance. We must recognize, of course, that the story of that development did not end in 1552 and there are necessary nuances to understand in both the 1559 and 1662 revisions. The amendments in 1559 were a light touch, part of the careful subtlety of the Elizabethan settlement. The Protestant basis of Anglican liturgy and identity were affirmed, and yet there were important adjustments. The Words of Administration of 1549 and 1552 were combined. This was hardly a return to a Catholic understanding, but represented the moderate hand of Elizabeth, keen as ever on both good order and royal supremacy.

The third trend, a lessening of medieval and Catholic apparel, is also seen. In the 1559 amendments the Black Rubric on kneeling was removed as unnecessary and the Ornaments Rubric was introduced. This latter has proved controversial to historians, due to ambiguity in what was actually meant by the reference to the vestments which were in use in the second year of the reign of Edward VI. The principle was that the vestments were to remain non-eucharistic (reinforcing the Protestant nature of the Elizabethan settlement); the detail had to be clarified in 1565 by Elizabeth's Archbishop, Matthew Parker, in his *Advertisements* decreeing that the clergy were to wear surplice and hood.

The amendments in 1662, following the restoration of Charles II, were also moderate and yet have also caused uncertainty. In concession to the Puritans, the Black Rubric on kneeling was restored, with a minor change in the wording, that some quite erroneously claim permits an understanding of real presence in the elements. It was never intended so. It was restored due to Puritan sensibilities. The Prayer Book of 1662, as in 1559, was based firmly upon the Protestant Prayer Book of 1552. The acceptance of the Prayer Book by many (though not all) of the Puritans is an indication that it was a reaffirmation of the Protestant nature of the liturgy rather than a step back in a more Catholic direction. It was the imposition of the Act of Corporation, requiring an oath repudiating the Commonwealth period, that drove large numbers reluctantly into nonconformity in the second round of the Great Ejection of 1662, discussed later in this chapter.

The Thirty-Nine Articles

During the course of Henry's reign various sets of Articles were produced. Part of the dilemma of the English Reformation was the extent to which the Reformed faith could, or should, be expressed in 'confessions of faith'. Some argued that the Creeds were sufficient, others that it was important for the Protestant faith to set down – in varying degrees of detail – its core beliefs. The English Reformation shows again its uniqueness by its adoption of the principle of a confession (it is simply inaccurate to claim that the Thirty-Nine Articles are not a confession of faith), but to do so with a distinctive Englishness in tone and content.

In 1536 the Ten Articles were drawn up, followed by the Bishops' Book in 1537 and the Thirteen Articles in 1538 (never published). The first two, in particular, were unremarkable statements. The latter, clearly showing the influence of the Lutheran Augsburg Confession, was an indication of Cranmer's slow but sure steps forward in defining the doctrinal boundaries of the Church of England. The Six Articles of 1539 were a step back, reasserting traditional Catholic doctrine. The battle, though, had moved into the area of confessions of faith. The King's Book of 1543 was the last statement of the rather tentative moves in this direction during Henry's reign. Unsurprisingly, things changed with the accession of Edward VI. In 1552 Cranmer tabled a series of Forty-Two Articles which formed the substance of the later Thirty-Nine Articles. Under Elizabeth, there was first the Eleven Articles of 1561, but then, in 1563, a revision of the Forty-Two Articles began. After a lengthy process involving the addition of four Articles, the omission of four and changes to 17 of the original Forty-Two, the Articles came to Convocation for approval. At this point three further Articles against Anabaptism were removed and the Queen herself removed one on the sacraments. The Articles were not submitted to Parliament for approval. In 1570 the Pope excommunicated Elizabeth. The rationale for a confession of faith of English Anglican Protestantism was very strong. Bishop John Jewel reworked the final version (re-inserting Article 29 removed by the Queen); the Articles were approved by Parliament in 1571 and have remained unchanged ever since.

The Articles are unmistakably Protestant. They are also shaped by the uniqueness of the English Reformation. The Articles show some influence of early Lutheranism but also, significantly, of continental Reformed Protestantism. The Articles strike a tone of moderate Calvinism. The chief architects were, apart from

Cranmer, Archbishop Matthew Parker and Bishop John Jewel, both ardent defenders of the Reformed Anglican settlement.

The Ordinal

The services of ordination set out a Church's beliefs in respect of ministry. What is the picture of ordained ministry painted by the Ordinal? In the preface, the Ordinal asserts the threefold ministry of bishop, priest and deacon. These orders are claimed to be 'evident unto all men diligently reading Holy Scripture and ancient Authors'.[21] In other words, the clarity of the threefold order, however valid, is not entirely clear from a plain reading of Scripture! This lack of clarity has been demonstrated in Anglican history by the way in which the diaconate has developed into a probationary period in modern Anglicanism, the basis for which is entirely unclear both biblically and historically. Similarly, the word priest is derived from the Greek *presbyteros*, translated in the New Testament as 'elder'.

In the 1552 Ordinal the services of ordination were described as the making of deacons, the ordaining of priests and the consecrating of bishops. In 1662 this distinction was reduced to ordaining (deacons and priests) and consecrating (bishops). The point is that there is a difference in *function* but not necessarily in *order* between a presbyter–priest and a bishop. The use of the description 'consecration' is intended to convey that the bishop is a senior presbyter, called and set aside for the particular responsibilities of oversight, rather than being ordained to a separate order of ministry. In the history of Anglicanism both points of view have had their claimants, but the ecclesiological implications for the understanding of the Church are significant. The later claims of the nature of episcopacy and of the Church, built up through the Caroline Divines (which we will consider shortly), but in particular the Oxford Movement, of the bishop being of the very essence of the Church, give weight to this understanding of ministry. It has a major impact today upon the way in which episcopal oversight is exercised and understood. It sits ill at ease with the foundation documents of Anglicanism. To the reform of episcopal leadership we will return.

The themes of the Ordinal set out a Reformed understanding of ministry. In the exhortation by the bishop, those called to be ordained are described as messengers, watchmen and stewards, called to teach and premonish (that is, to admonish), to feed and provide. They are called upon to seek the lost sheep and to treasure those committed to their charge, bought with the blood of Christ. They are called to be studious in the Scriptures; to live lives consonant with the Scriptures, which they should read and weigh daily; and that they should be wholesome and godly examples to the flock. In the declarations, made by those to be ordained, candidates acknowledge the authority of the Bible, commit themselves to living the Christian life, to driving away false teaching and to be diligent in study and prayer. The picture is a great one and a dynamic one. It is part of the core heritage of Anglicanism which has become obscured and disguised. Indeed, as we will note subsequently, confusion over the nature of the ministry can lead to tension. The vision, though, of a glorious heritage of ministry, to watch, to teach and to live the Scriptures, is one both worthy of recovery and one of which Anglicanism can be proud.

Excursus – the Prayer Books of Edward VI and The Thirty-Nine Articles

As noted in the commentary, the Prayer Book of 1549 made some enormous steps. It was designed to indicate reform in both the content and the externals of the liturgy. In terms of eucharistic doctrine, emphasis on the reception of the elements (rather than their consecration, though that was still retained) was introduced for the first time. Regarding externals, the medieval Mass vestment – the chasuble – was replaced by the cope: traditionally a non-eucharistic garment. Even in 1549 the Protestantism of the English Reformation was stirring within the liturgy and practice of the English Church.

Comparing the Prayer Books of 1549 and 1552
The developments with the Prayer Book of 1552 are well illustrated by considering what was added and subtracted from the 1549 book.

Additions to 1549:
- The Ten Commandments
- The Words of Administration
- The phrase, 'militant here in earth' to the prayer for the Church
- The Black Rubric

These additions were exceptionally important. The Ten Commandments reinforced the moral teaching of Scripture rather than the Church. The Words of Administration demonstrated categorically that the high point of the service was the moment of the reception of the elements by the believer. In 1549 these words read as follows:

> The body of our Lord Jesus Christ, which was given for thee, preserve thy body and soul unto everlasting life.

In 1552 these became:

> Take and eat this in remembrance that Christ died for thee, and feed on him in thy heart by faith, with thanksgiving.

Remembrance of Christ's death, feeding in the heart, joyfully and with thanks and by faith, became the focus of Communion.

The addition of the phrase 'militant here in earth' in the prayer for the Church was a specific insertion to counter any possible suggestion of prayers for the dead.

The Protestant emphasis of 1552 was further reinforced by the addition of the Black Rubric, making clear that kneeling at the administration of the elements was not to be taken in any way to imply adoration of the elements themselves. The bread and wine 'remain still in their very natural substances' and as regards 'the natural body and blood of our Saviour Christ, they are in heaven and not here', closely reflecting Zwingli's position. The 'rubric' was inserted late, by order of the Council, with the book already at the printers; kneeling was to be required, but this was not to imply presence or adoration.

Deletions from 1549:

- The invocation of the Holy Spirit upon the elements
- Mention of the faithful departed
- References to 'memorial' from the prayer of thanksgiving
- Versicles and responses around the gospel reading

Again the movement is clear. The invocation of the Spirit upon the elements was removed because the Spirit was in the hearts of the believers. All the above deletions point towards a united view of Scripture, a Protestant eucharistic doctrine and a core element of Anglican identity.

The Thirty-Nine Articles

The Articles can be grouped in a number of ways. One classic manner is as follows:

A   The substance of faith (Articles I–V)
B   The rule of faith (Articles VI–VIII)
C   The life of faith, or personal religion (Articles IX–XVIII)
D   The household of faith or corporate religion (Articles XIX–XXXIX)

Section D can then be further sub-divided:

(i)   The Church (Articles XIX–XXII)
(ii)   The ministry (Articles XXIII–XXIV)
(iii)   The sacraments (Articles XXV–XXXI)
(iv)   Church discipline (Articles XXXII–XXXIX)
(v)   Church and state (Articles XXXVII–XXXIX)

Example extracts:

Article 1   Of faith in the Holy Trinity
There is but one living and true God, everlasting, without body, parts or passions, of infinite power, wisdom, and goodness, the Maker and Preserver of all things, both visible and invisible. And in unity of this Godhead there be three

Persons, of one substance, power, and eternity, the Father, the Son and the Holy Ghost.

Article 6   Of the sufficiency of the holy Scriptures for salvation
Holy Scripture containeth all things necessary to salvation: so that whatsoever is not read therein, nor may be proved thereby, is not to be required of any man, that it should be believed as an article of the Faith, or be thought requisite or necessary to salvation. In the name of the holy Scripture we do understand those canonical books of the Old and New Testament, of whose authority was never any doubt in the Church.

Article 17   Of predestination and election (part)
Predestination to life is the everlasting purpose of God, whereby (before the foundations of the world were laid) he hath constantly decreed by his counsel secret to us, to deliver from curse and damnation those whom he has chosen in Christ out of mankind, and to bring them by Christ to everlasting salvation, as vessels made to honour . . .

Article 28   Of the Lord's Supper
The Supper of the Lord is not only a sign of the love that Christians ought to have among themselves one to another; but rather is a sacrament of our redemption by Christ's death: insomuch that to such as rightly, worthily, and with faith, receive the same, the bread which we break is a partaking of the Body of Christ; and likewise the cup of blessing is a partaking of the Blood of Christ.

Transubstantiation (or the change of the substance of bread and wine) in the Supper of the Lord, cannot be proved by holy Writ; but is repugnant to the plain words of Scripture, overthroweth the nature of a sacrament, and hath given occasion to many superstitions.

The Body of Christ is given, taken, and eaten, in the Supper, only after an heavenly and spiritual manner. And the means whereby the Body of Christ is received and eaten in the Supper is faith.

The sacrament of the Lord's Supper was not by Christ's ordinance reserved, carried about, lifted up, or worshipped.

Commentary

The history of the Articles is described in the main text. The examples drawn out above illustrate the nature of the Articles. They begin with confession of a common Trinitarian faith, compatible with the Creeds as well as the Scriptures, consistent with Catholic teaching in its truest sense (the common teaching of the universal Church). We see also, in Article 6, the whole basis of authority within Anglicanism, a matter to which we will return. We see the influence of the continental Reformation in Article 17 with a clear commitment of Anglicanism to predestination, albeit with emphasis upon predestination to life. Article 28, dealing with the Lord's Supper, illustrates both the clarity of the Reformed teaching on the Eucharist and the distinctiveness of Cranmer's emphasis on receptionism. There is a hint of anti-Roman Catholicism at the end which is reflected in a number of the other Articles. The Church of England with its formation under Henry and Edward and development in the time of Elizabeth, is founded upon both the clarity and the distinctiveness of the Reformation settlement in England.

Anglican influences from Elizabeth to the Enlightenment

If the foundations are so clearly Protestant and Reformed, albeit with nuances here and there, how has the obscuring of this heritage occurred? What is the basis of the other Anglican traditions and the building blocks which have gone into their development? Are there aspects which can be seen as essential to Anglicanism and what elements might be seen as part of Anglicanism's rich variety but not its core? Many in the more liberal tradition of Anglicanism, especially those within the Enlightenment tradition of rationality, do indeed lay claim to a definitive Anglican tradition. Many of these influences derive from the eighteenth and nineteenth centuries with their challenges to authority, tradition and meaning. There is almost a revelling in the certainty of uncertainty. There are a number of important theological names and movements which go together to form the foundations of this approach. However, before considering these influences, there are important additional building blocks from Elizabeth's reign.

The Elizabethan settlement and John Jewel

Elizabeth reigned from 1558 to 1603, a fact of considerable significance after short periods on the throne for Edward VI (1547–1553) and Mary Tudor (1553–1558). She had a remarkable influence upon the consolidation of the Reformation settlement and the future shape of the Church of England. Elizabeth was the daughter of Henry and Anne Boleyn – there would be no return to Rome. The Elizabethan settlement is much discussed and claimed in support of numerous positions. The settlement itself consisted of an Act of Supremacy (which stated the case against Rome and restored the cup to the laity) and the Act of Uniformity (which imposed the amended Prayer Book). Subsequently, Elizabeth removed pro-Catholic bishops and all the bishops selected by Elizabeth were firmly in favour of the Protestant Reformation settlement, some having been in exile, though others, including Archbishop Matthew Parker and Bishop John Jewel, had conformed under Mary. Like all monarchs, Elizabeth was concerned for the royal supremacy and this as much as anything else led her to resist the demands of the Puritans: those within the Church pressing for further reform in the direction of Calvin's Geneva including, ultimately, the abolition of the episcopate. Some modern Anglicans have sought to present the Elizabethan period as a *via media* between Rome and Geneva. Nothing could be further from the reality. Elizabeth, through her bishops, established a thoroughly Reformed Church of England, with an episcopal leadership designed to reflect, in both its belief and practice, this English Reformed Protestantism. The settlement set the English Church once and for all over and against Rome. The composition of the episcopate, the adoption (largely) of the 1552 Prayer Book and the development of the Thirty-Nine Articles all clearly set out the stance of the Church of England. Elizabeth had no need, and little time, for Puritan demands. Not only were they a threat, but their demands were simply unnecessary because Elizabeth had established a Reformed episcopal Church – and, naturally, maintained the royal supremacy.

John Jewel is an excellent example of an Elizabethan bishop. Returning to England upon Elizabeth's accession to the throne, he was quickly appointed to the See of Salisbury in 1558 (indicating Elizabeth's Protestant intentions). Jewel was a passionate defender of the Reformation settlement in England, an advocate of the Reformed Church of England and one of the few bishops who sought to lead and serve their dioceses in holy living and godly example. Jewel could perhaps be described as an 'episcopal Calvinist'. He was sympathetic to many of the Puritan demands, but regretted that so many of his friends joined the Puritan party. Jewel tussled with those responsible for the Puritan *Admonition* of 1572 (a Puritan manifesto – discussed later). The Church of England, he argued, was a fully Reformed Church, with a Reformed episcopate. It stood against Rome and its catholicity depended upon apostolicity. In other words, its unity and universality was based upon the teaching of the apostles – content rather than form.

He set out his arguments in his *Apology of the Church in England*, published in Latin in 1562 and English in 1564, together with his *Defence of the Apology*, first published in 1568 and in enlarged form in 1570. The *Apology* has six sections. The first deals with the claims of Protestantism as defender of truth. The second sets out the Reformed understanding of the Anglican formularies, over and against Rome, not least in respect of ministry and the Lord's Supper. In the third section, Jewel claims that it is the Protestant Reformers who, despite errors, such as Anabaptism, stand in true succession to the Fathers and Councils and of the early Church. In his fourth section he exposes Rome and its claims and in the fifth denies the Roman claim to antiquity. The final section denies the validity of the Council of Trent.[22] Jewel positioned himself explicitly on the grounds of the authority of Scripture; however, he also sought to argue with the Roman position on its own terms. Hence Jewel appealed to the patristic Fathers and Councils. This was not to invest them with authority, but rather to illustrate that it was the Protestant Reformation rather than Rome who were their true inheritors. From 1560 onwards Jewel devoted himself to his diocese, with efforts to improve parochial life, preaching and encouraging charity. He lived a modest lifestyle – contrary to many in episcopal office. He was a patron of the young Richard Hooker.

Richard Hooker

Richard Hooker (1554–1600) is claimed by all Anglican traditions as part of their heritage. Partially this is because Hooker's principal writing was a defence of Anglican polity, a rational apology for Anglican forms of government, the defence of festivals and ceremonies as 'matters indifferent', as well as being a work of systematic theology. A key question in understanding Hooker is whether he was writing up a *via media* between Geneva and Rome (or Canterbury and Rome, or even Canterbury and Geneva, depending upon the position adopted) or whether his purpose was primarily a defence of the Protestant Elizabethan settlement, though not least against the Puritan pressure for further reform. Rowan Williams comments that 'Hooker – like the Anglican tradition as a whole, it is tempting to add – is tantalizingly hard to pigeonhole'.[23] Hooker's major theological work, *Of the Laws of Ecclesiastical Polity*, was published from 1593 onwards. This masterpiece consisted of eight books, five of which were published in his lifetime. There is particular suspicion that Book VII, which praised the powers of bishops with far more enthusiasm than his earlier writings, was doctored. Book VII was published in 1662. The Act of Uniformity around the Prayer Book of Charles II generated plenty of vested interests claiming Hooker in defence of the Anglican establishment, as will be noted later.

Hooker, in Book V, together with his *Discourse on Justification*, illustrates his conviction that salvation comes through Jesus Christ, that it is unmerited, and that at the moment of justification the gift of the Holy Spirit is received, and justification made real. For Hooker the sacraments are means of participation in Christ; he was not interested in discussing whether the bread and wine changed. For him the consecration lay in the use. Hooker was clearly setting out a Reformed framework of doctrinal understanding. Hooker argued that tradition had a valuable role to play in those areas of church life upon which Scripture was silent. The Puritans were in error to oppose tradition when Scripture did not speak. The value of the customs and traditions of the visible Church were not limited to the validation of Scripture. The Church of England had separated from Rome because Rome was in error, rather than because Rome was 'the whore of Babylon', the anti-Christ. Hence there was the need for great moderation in retaining many traditional practices. Extending this argument, Hooker thus saw distinctively positive value in the structures and ordering of the Church of England in line with ancient tradition. So aspects of polity which the Puritans held out as 'remnants of popery' Hooker proclaimed as 'badges of honour'. Hooker emphasized:

- Public prayer, liturgy and sacraments
- Festivals and some ceremonial (in context of times)
- Role of episcopate – though not as *divine right*; the Church could legitimately divest itself

It is easy to see how different traditions have come to appeal to Hooker. It is important to note both his central purpose and the variety around that core to which differing traditions have appealed.

The Caroline Divines

Given the importance for the English Church of royal supremacy, it is inevitable that the character and intentions of the monarch for the time being should shape in a significant way the direction of the Church during their particular reign. In the period after Elizabeth, especially as first James I (1603–1625) and then Charles I (1625–1649) rose to power, there developed an increasing dichotomy between Charles' episcopate and the increasingly dominant Puritans in Parliament. During this period a number of prominent episcopal leaders, together with other writers, developed a particular understanding of the Anglican tradition. This group has become known as the Caroline Divines. Their leaders were Lancelot Andrewes (1555–1626), Bishop of Winchester from 1618; John Cosin (1594–1672), Bishop of Durham from 1660; Jeremy Taylor (1613–1667), one-time chaplain to Charles I; George Herbert (1593–1633), poet and priest; and Nicholas Ferrar (1592–1637), founder of the Little Gidding community. They thrived under William Laud (1573–1645), Archbishop from 1633 until his execution under an Act of Attainder in 1645.

The characteristics of the Caroline Divines were these:

- An elevated sense of royal supremacy
- A 'high' view of the Church and the episcopate
- A claim to primitive catholicity
- Emphasis on the *via media* between Rome and Geneva
- A higher view of form and beauty in worship
- A more Catholic view of the Eucharist
- A developed spirituality and poetry

Two things should be noted by way of assessment. First, the departure from the Reformed Anglicanism of Jewel. The enhanced sense of royal supremacy and the episcopate was now detached from the Reformed Anglican position of the Elizabethan years. Hence, rather than establishing their position against both Rome and the Puritan demands, the Carolines set themselves against the Puritans but without the bulwark of a clearly defined Reformed Anglican understanding. This led to the rather vague view of Anglicanism as the *via media* between two extremes. Second, there is the importance of this group of divines for later High Churchmanship. This is especially so for the non-jurors[24] of the eighteenth century (e.g. William Law), but also as part of the claim of the Oxford Movement for continuity back through Anglican history into the period of blessedness of the early Church. The Carolines were an important part of Anglican history, but their understanding and position were closely affected by the political realities they faced. They made excellent contributions to the development of spirituality and poetry in an age when such was frowned upon in the religious context. However, the weight that they are sometimes expected to bear by others pays little regard to their place in the bigger story and often owes more to the romanticism of the later historian than it does to the historical reality.

Anglicanism and the Enlightenment

The Enlightenment describes a philosophical movement which emerged during the eighteenth century. Key philosophers such as Locke, Leibniz, Voltaire and Kant were all part of the movement. It was the Age of Reason. The implications of this intellectual current for theology have been enormous. Enlightenment thinking has been characterized by:

- An emphasis on reason
- The importance of the natural order
- The idea of progress
- Rejection of the authority of both revelation and tradition

This movement first of all influenced deists (belief in a non-personal supreme being) and freethinkers (more radical), but in time it also came to affect Christian theology. What was the place of reason in Christian thought? The development of Enlightenment ideas in continental Europe had a particular impact upon German theology. One area was biblical criticism, applying the tools of the Enlightenment to the nature, content and composition of the Bible. Thus the nineteenth century saw various quests for the historical Jesus, seeking, through critical method, to disentangle, as it was seen, the facts about Jesus from later glosses and commentary. Source criticism (analysis of pre-final text source material) and form criticism (assessment of the various forms of literary text) were applied to the Bible. Similarly, scientific method was applied to the understanding of humanity – as well as to the first chapters of Genesis – and so the previously generally accepted Christian worldview came to be challenged, within as well as without the Church. This was all a tremendous shock to the world of faith and many reacted with horror.

However, the movement positively impacted on Anglican theologians from F. D. Maurice, B. F. Westcott and Charles Kingsley to Charles Gore. Maurice (1805–1872) advocated the universal brotherhood of man under the eternal Fatherhood of God; he accepted the sincerity of other faiths and denied eternal punishment. This showed the clear influence of Enlightenment thought and it cost Maurice his Chair at King's College, London. We shall return to his influence in Chapter 4. Westcott (1825–1901), scholar and bishop, was associated with the Revised Version of the Bible which appeared in 1881. Knowledge about the text underlying the Bible was increasing through the publication of codices such as the *Codex Sinaiticus*. However, it was a much more significant step to acknowledge that the King James Bible contained inferior textual material; biblical authority itself was at stake. According to Westcott, Scripture was a field in which to exercise and to grow spiritually; to systematize and to idolize the text as a finished set of solutions was to reject the true gift.

Thus the foundations of modern liberal and liberal Catholic Anglicanism were laid in the reflections of modern critical scholarship, a rejection of literal interpretations of the Bible, scepticism about the supernatural and an increasing theological emphasis on the incarnation. All of this was expressed in a variety of ways and, of course, provoked a range of reactions, but these ideas formed a very strong strand of the Anglican tradition in the century following 1870. In this, the foundations were also laid for major Anglican names of the twentieth century, including Michael Ramsey, John Robinson and Rowan Williams, who, in slightly different ways, represent the modern inheritance of both Catholic and liberal traditions within Anglicanism.

Anglicanism in the New World

The foundations of Anglicanism across the world are the same, but their course and development have been varied. The Church of England, together with the Book of Common Prayer, landed in North America with the colonists and between 1607 (Virginia) and 1758 (Georgia) became the established Church of the colonies. The ministry was provided by the Bishop of London, working through commissaries. Pressure for an American bishop led to tension in the period before independence. Some welcomed the strengthening of the link to England, others were apprehensive of any movement towards episcopacy. In 1775 the Church was disestablished throughout the colonies and achieved formal independence from the Church of England in 1789. In 1784 Samuel Seabury, elected Bishop of Connecticut, sought consecration in England but found the Oath of Supremacy insurmountable. He was therefore consecrated by 'non-juring' Scottish bishops. Two years later William White and Samuel Provoost were consecrated in England. In 1789 a constitution was adopted and the first American Book of Common Prayer was published, mainly the 1662 Prayer Book, but with some Scottish influence. Major revisions took place in 1928 and 1979. This historical background has affected the Episcopal Church of the USA in a number of ways.

Dissent: from Puritanism to Anglo-Catholic varieties

Dissent takes many forms and is expressed in a wide variety of ways. The establishment, that is, the prevailing presumption within Anglicanism of ecclesiastical and cultural norms at any one time, has vested interest in defining dissent from those norms as lying outside the Anglican framework. It is surprising how prevalent such attitudes are. A proper perspective to Anglicanism requires further enquiry into the breadth and nature of dissent within the Anglican tradition.

Royal supremacy maintained Elizabeth's suspicion of the Puritans. In 1558, the year of Mary's death and Elizabeth's accession, John Knox published a missive challenging the right of women to rule: *The First Blast of the Trumpet against the monstrous regiment of women.* Elizabeth was not amused. What then did the Puritan dissenters in the reign of Elizabeth press for? Three areas in particular:

- Abolition of the episcopate (in favour of the Geneva offices of deacon, elder, etc.)
- Separation of Church and state
- Doctrinal purity

The Puritans effectively wanted further and continued reform. They made a number of steps forward in their demands. There had been, from the Puritan perspective, much progress in terms of doctrine not least in the areas of predestination and eucharistic doctrine, as well as in much of the external peripherals such as ecclesiastical dress (though the Puritans opposed the surplice). The Elizabethan Puritans lived with much of the ambiguity of the Prayer Book, but the point of contention came with the requirement in 1571 to subscribe to the Articles of Religion, the oath of subscription containing the assertion that the Book of Common Prayer contained *nothing* against the Word of God. The Church of England had managed to maintain a doctrinal core whilst a degree of variety was always tolerated. The testing points came in 1571, in 1662 and in 1688 with subscription to various oaths requiring clergy to abjure particular positions upon pain of ejection from their livings.

The Puritan position can be illustrated by this extract from *An*

Admonition to the Parliament, submitted to Parliament by John Field and Thomas Wilcox in 1572:

> . . . we have at all times borne with that which we could not amend in this book and have used the same in our ministry, so far forth as we might . . . yet now being compelled by subscription to allow the same and to confess it not to be against the word of God in any point, but tolerable, we must needs say as followeth that this book is an imperfect book, culled and picked out of that popish dunghill . . . For some and many of the contents therein be such as are against the word of God.

It is difficult, and not entirely advisable, to use our modern eyes to interpret what is being said. Noteworthy is the recognition that even the Puritans – continuing as ministers within the framework of the Church of England – accepted the variety around the core of the Prayer Book tradition. It was seeing the book as 'not against the word of God in any point' that caused the dissension. In our modern day, to assert that the Book of Common Prayer is imperfect would seem an uncontroversial point, though few would then indulge in the dramatic, flowery sub-clause that follows with its language of anti-Catholicism, despite something of a heritage of anti-Catholicism within Evangelical identity.

Elizabeth resisted the Puritans while never once loosening her basic Protestant disposition; she was concerned for good and godly order as much as she was for theology. A further complexity is the role of the royal supremacy as a factor in assessing both the core and the variety of Anglicanism. Dissent from royal supremacy has come from a number of different directions in Anglican history, as has its defence. Throughout the history of the Church of England there has also been both a persecution of Puritan divines and yet also a continuing presence within the Church of those of Puritan disposition. Indeed the same could be said, as will be illustrated subsequently, of those of Catholic leaning.

Another period of dissent within the history of the Church of England is that of the Restoration (1660) following the Commonwealth (1649–1660). A detailed analysis of the period 1633–1660 is not possible. However, during that time we see both the Laudian response to Elizabethan Protestantism and the Cromwellian experiment in Church and state. If Laud was concerned for royal supremacy, church order and ceremonial above doctrine, then Cromwell not only imposed a legalistic Puritanism but he also effectively adopted the mantle of royal supremacy itself. Cromwell himself generated further dissent from more radical elements. In 1660, as the godly Commonwealth crumbled, the monarchy was restored under Charles II. Immediately, Charles re-established the episcopate and then, in 1662, a modestly revised Prayer Book, albeit, as we have noted, with some concessions to the Puritans. For a hard core of 700 clergy this was all too much and they departed at once from their livings. An Act of Uniformity required subscription to the Prayer Book. In line with the tradition of the Elizabethan Puritans, many godly Puritan ministers were willing to accept this, albeit 'an imperfect book'. However, a Corporation Act also required an oath repudiating Cromwell's Commonwealth and supporting the royal supremacy. This was too much for even Richard Baxter, 'the reluctant nonconformist',[25] and on St Bartholomew's Day 1662 the Great Ejection was completed with an additional 1,000 clergy, Baxter included, ejected from their livings. Yet, there were Puritan clergy who remained. An important question in the identity of Anglicanism is that of how central is the notion of royal supremacy and what does it really mean in practice? Historically, the more particular has been the definition of royal supremacy, the narrower has been the Anglican identity – on a global basis, such a narrow emphasis on royal supremacy is unjustifiable.

A different example illustrates the point from another direction. Following the reigns of Charles II and James II, who eventually fled into exile in 1688, the Protestant William of Orange together with his wife, Mary, were invited to assume the throne. The reign of the House of Stuart, with all its ambiguities and its religious preferences with at least half an eye to Rome, was over. The new ruling house was, like every other dynasty, keen to establish itself and ensure both order and compliance. So, unsurprisingly, an Act of Uniformity was introduced requiring oaths repudiating the Stuarts. Equally unsurprising there was dissent; this time from the very clergy who had supported the Stuarts. Those who refused the oath of 1688 were known as non-jurors. They continued, as many Puritans before them had continued, to minister in their parishes. One notable example of the non-juring tradition of 1688 is William Law. He quietly produced devotional works, including *A Serious Call to a Devout and Holy Life*, that had considerable influence upon John Wesley. Why did Law refuse the oath? Partly loyalty, partly adherence to the doctrines of the divine rule of kings, partly a particular concern for church order. Here we have the origins of an orthodox High Churchmanship. Devotion, order, Church, episcopacy were its hallmarks. A concern for holiness of life was its currency. It built on the Caroline tradition and in turn was appealed to by the Anglo-Catholic revival of the nineteenth century. It also played a part in the backdrop to the Evangelical Revival. The Evangelical Revival itself we will look at in detail in the next chapter. For the moment let us turn to the Catholic revival of the mid-nineteenth century.

The Oxford Movement has had a significant influence upon the spirituality and shape of today's Church of England. The movement comes with its own heroes and house histories (written from the inside as apologies for the movement), its own spirituality, theology and worship, its own followers and successors. Yet most scholars assert that the Oxford Movement itself represents a significant discontinuity in the historical understanding of the Church of England, a serious misreading of the religious history of England in the sixteenth century.[26] Equally, we cannot deny both the presence and the continuing influence of those who derive their spiritual history from the Oxford Movement. It is not adequate to declare this tradition as not Anglican, as also when levelled, without qualification, at the Puritans.

The movement originated in intellectual theological quests for a united, spiritual, Catholic Church, indeed a Church separated from the influence of the state. It is not accurate to see the origins of Anglo-Catholicism in ritual and ceremony; that came later. The foundation documents of the Church, even the Thirty-Nine Articles, could not be allowed to stand in the way. The height of the quest was Tract 90, one of a series of *Tracts for the Times*, setting out the vision of Catholic revival and renewal. This was the last of the Tracts, the author being John Henry Newman. The Thirty-Nine Articles were uncomfortable to the Oxford clerics and their followers (often referred to, rather disparagingly, as Puseyites, after the Oxford don, Edward Pusey). The Articles, in their strictures against cults and the authority of the papacy, and in the tone of the Articles on justification, authority and sacraments, were seen as at increasing variance from their understanding of the Catholic faith. Tract 90 was published on 27 February 1841 with the explicit aim of arguing that those of Catholic disposition could faithfully subscribe to the Articles:

> It is often urged, and sometimes felt and granted, that there are in the Articles propositions or terms inconsistent with the Catholic faith . . . The following Tract is drawn up with the view of showing how groundless the objection is . . . our articles also, the offspring of an uncatholic age, are, through God's good providence, to say the least, not uncatholic, and may be subscribed by those who aim at being catholic in heart and doctrine.[27]

Although at this stage Newman still believed that Rome was in error, it was a watershed. For Newman the road to Rome was to become the only one down which he could travel. Newman bemused many by his attempts to develop a Catholic understanding apart from Roman Catholicism, contrary to the plain meaning of the Articles, especially in his convoluted attempts to explain away the Articles on purgatory and the Mass. At Oxford itself the Tract was censured by the Heads of Houses.

From around 1845 onwards a second period of Anglo-Catholic dissent developed as the Catholic renewal movement took on a more explicit mantle of 'ritualism'. Catholic-minded clergy introduced forms of apparel and services which sought to demonstrate the Catholic authenticity of Anglican ministry and worship. Hence, the use of incense, candles, genuflection, vestments, intoning, the title 'Father', adoration of the elements of Communion and even developments such as the clerical collar became more prominent in some places. As well as provoking negative reaction from Evangelicals and the wider Protestant movement (such things were viewed as a combination of doctrinally suspect and 'un-English'), there was also, initially, resistance from the bishops, not least in respect of authority.

Briefly, it is also pertinent to mention the development of Christian socialism as another aspect of dissent within Anglicanism, deriving part of its heritage from both Catholic and liberal elements of the tradition. This was expressed in a number of ways. First, through the emergence of 'slum priests', Catholic-minded clergy determined to bring the richness of Catholic ceremonial and ritual to the poor, alongside evangelistic zeal and preaching. Second, through the theological influences of F. D. Maurice. Third, through a range of groups and organizations such as the Christian Social Union (CSU). We will return to this topic in Chapter 4. The Episcopal Church of the USA is linked to some of the dissenting expressions of Anglicanism, its independence having been partly secured through the non-juring tradition. Indeed, it is perhaps inevitably so, given the nature of the founding of the New World and subsequent independence. This gave rise to the Episcopal Church having to position itself more particularly in the marketplace. The Oxford Movement had considerable impact and, as we shall see in Chapter 3, actually led to a split, which did not occur in England.

Authority in Anglicanism: from the Bible to bishops

What then are the sources of authority in Anglicanism and what place is occupied by the Bible? The trinity of 'scripture, reason and tradition' has come to be seen as the determinative constituents of the Anglican tradition,[28] although both the basis and the implied equality are open to question. This mantra has been described as 'a train able to stop at every station and always add one more carriage. There is practically nothing it cannot accommodate'.[29] It can be seen that at differing times various expressions of Anglicanism have appealed to different elements of authority, indeed have placed differing weight upon Scripture, reason and tradition. The picture is, of course, much more nuanced than different traditions appealing to different sources, but it is important to understand both the core elements of authority within Anglicanism and the variety around that core. There are a number of building blocks.

Article 6

Article 6 Of the sufficiency of the holy Scriptures for salvation
Holy Scripture containeth all things necessary for salvation: so that whatsoever is not read therein, nor may be proved thereby, is not to be required of any man, that it should be believed as an article of the Faith, or be thought requisite or necessary to salvation. In the name of the holy Scripture we do understand those canonical books of the Old and New Testament, of whose authority was never any doubt in the Church.

The starting place is Scripture. The Article asserts both the sufficiency of Scripture and its authority. It also emphasizes the canonicity and the primacy of Scripture. The authority for both salvation and faith lies in Scripture and Scripture alone. This was a crucial emphasis of the Reformation right from the beginning of Luther's rediscovery or reassertion of the idea of justification by grace through faith. There is nothing that can be added to the requirements of Scripture for our salvation – nothing. It is, therefore, reasonable, if somewhat controversial, to assert that those elements of the Anglican tradition which have sought either to add to Scripture or to diminish the role of Scripture or to detach the Anglican understanding of Scripture from its moorings in the Reformation cannot be seen as belonging to the core of the Anglican tradition. The primacy of Scripture is illustrated or at least implied by the canonicity of the Old and New Testaments depending upon the prior authority of Scripture rather than the Church. This is not to 'unchurch' elements of the Anglican tradition which have brought differing emphases; simply to reassert what lies at the heart of Anglicanism rather than its periphery. Article 6, with Hooker, Jewel and the mainstream Anglican tradition, does not assert that the Church may only undertake or form itself in manners or ways that are expressly commanded in the Scriptures. The Bible is the standard of faith, the sole authority, an authority and standard of the first order; in other words a standard from which our salvation is derived. Second-order issues are left open by the Article. So while some elements of the Puritan tradition within Anglicanism invested second-order issues with scriptural authority, so also some Anglo-Catholic and liberal parts of Anglicanism placed other authorities alongside the Scriptures. Both these elements form at least part of the variety of Anglicanism, but neither can claim to represent its core identity.

The Chicago–Lambeth Quadrilateral

The origins of this declaration lie in its adoption by the House of Bishops in the Protestant Episcopal Church of the United States of America in 1886 and then, in slightly amended form, by the Lambeth Conference of 1888. Its contents, order and variety are all instructive.

Lambeth Conference of 1888, Resolution II

That, in the opinion of this Conference, the following Articles supply a basis on which approach may be, by God's blessing, made towards Home Reunion:

1 The Holy Scriptures of the Old and New Testaments as 'containing all things necessary to salvation', and as being the rule and ultimate standard of faith.
2 The Apostles' Creed, as the Baptismal Symbol; and the Nicene Creed, as the sufficient statement of the Christian faith.
3 The two Sacraments, ordained by Christ Himself – Baptism and the Supper of the Lord – ministered with unfailing use of Christ's words of Institution, and of the elements ordained by Him.
4 The Historic Episcopate, locally adapted in the methods of its administration to the varying needs of the nations and peoples called of God into the Unity of His Church.

This statement was produced as a basis for the reunion of the Churches. It dealt primarily with the first-order issues of the catholicity of the Church, the universal principles of faith – a confession of faith – upon which Christian unity can be based. Scripture came first. Article 6 was repeated and the description added that Scripture is 'the rule and ultimate standard of faith'. This made explicit what was implicit in Article 6, that there is a concern with authority as well as with the means of salvation. The catholicity of the Church is affirmed in the two Creeds of the Church, as a sufficient statement of the Christian faith, under Scripture. The basis of any unity, however, is to be upon the confession of a common faith. Anglicanism cannot be separated from such confession. Similarly, the two dominical sacraments (that is, those commanded in Scripture) are affirmed, reaffirming the Reformed understanding of the sacraments of baptism and the Lord's Supper, rather than any broader Catholic position. The theology of the sacraments is not explored, but the basis of both is Christ himself and the Words of Institution are to be those used by Christ. The reference is to the Lord's Supper, not the Mass or the Eucharist or even the Holy Communion. The theological basis is there for all to see. The fourth statement, dealing with the historic episcopate, may seem rather odd. Why introduce a matter of church order into such a statement of confession? Is this asserting the indispensability of the historic episcopate as received within Anglicanism as of the very essence of the Church, a defining characteristic? Closer examination bears fruit. The principles of episcopacy are apostolicity, oversight, order and unity. The declaration implicitly asserts these principles rather than the exact form of the episcopate. The principles of the apostolic faith have already been laid down; no form of church order is to have priority over these. The principle rather is that of oversight achieved through the episcopate being adapted locally according to the needs of the people. This could not be further from any Anglican imperialism. The principles of episcopacy are asserted as prior to its form.

Canon A5

This canon sets out the identity of Anglicanism.

> *Canon A5   Of the doctrine of the Church of England*
> The doctrine of the Church of England is grounded in the Holy Scriptures, and in such teachings of the ancient Fathers and Councils of the Church as are agreeable to the said Scriptures.
>   In particular such doctrine is to be found in the Thirty-nine Articles of Religion, *The Book of Common Prayer*, and the Ordinal.

The principles of Canon A5 are clear and consistent with everything which has so far been claimed for authority within Anglicanism. The primacy of Scripture is asserted. The very basis of the Church of England belongs in the Scriptures. Tradition – set out here as the teachings of the ancient Fathers and Councils of the Church – is affirmed only insofar as such teachings agree with the Scriptures. The biblical doctrine as applied to the Church of England is asserted to lie in the formularies; the Thirty-Nine

Articles, the Book of Common Prayer and the Ordinal. These three are to be seen as in agreement with each other and all three as consonant with the Scriptures. There is no room here for claiming either the equality of Scripture and Tradition, or for claiming that Protestant Articles balance a Catholic Prayer Book.

The Declaration of Assent

Upon being made deacon, ordained presbyter or consecrated bishop, together with any occasion upon which a new appointment is taken up, the Declaration of Assent is made. The detailed history of the Declaration, its genesis, issues of subscription and its journey through the synodical process are set out elsewhere.[30] During its development the proposed Declaration was amended in a number of distinct ways in the process of revision. This had the effect of more closely allying the Declaration with the historic Anglican understanding of the Scriptures and the Articles. After the Trinitarian introduction, the wording was eventually strengthened to indicate that this common faith was *professed* by the Church of England, and uniquely *revealed* in the Holy Scriptures and set forth in the Catholic Creeds, again illustrating primacy to Scripture, the role of the Creeds being to set out faithfully what has been revealed in Scripture. As we have seen, this was a sufficient statement of the common faith, but only insofar as the Creeds were agreeable to the Scriptures.

It is very difficult to take this range of documents, together with the historic formularies themselves, and maintain that the reference to 'proclaim afresh in each generation' implies any change from the basic primacy and authority of Scripture. After the assertion of the common faith, the particular distinctive of the Church of England is set out in the references to the Articles, the Prayer Book and the Ordinal. These are secondary matters, dependent upon and derived from the primacy of Scripture and its unique revelation of the faith. They belong together, not apart, and represent the setting out of the confessional framework of Anglicanism in its doctrinal Articles, affirmed in the doctrines conveyed in the Prayer Book and the manner of its orders of ministries. The claim, by Colin Podmore, that in the Declaration of Assent 'The Church of England is given no denominational or confessional description',[31] must be treated with considerable caution.

The Declaration of Assent

Preface
The Church of England is part of the One, Holy, Catholic and Apostolic Church worshipping the one true God, Father, Son and Holy Spirit. She professes the faith uniquely revealed in the Holy Scriptures and set forth in the catholic creeds, which faith the Church is called upon to proclaim afresh in each generation. Led by the Holy Spirit, she has borne witness to Christian truth in her historic formularies, the Thirty-nine Articles of Religion, the Book of Common Prayer and the Ordering of Bishops, Priests and Deacons. In the declaration you are about to make will you affirm your loyalty to this inheritance of faith as your inspiration and guidance under God in bringing the grace and truth of Christ to this generation and making Him known to those in your care?

Declaration of Assent
I, A B, do so affirm, and accordingly declare my belief in the faith which is revealed in the Holy Scriptures and set forth in the catholic creeds and to which the historic formularies of the Church of England bear witness; and in public prayer and administration of the sacraments, I will use only the forms of service which are authorised or allowed by Canon.

To what extent is variation from these historic norms acceptable? How Anglican is it to hold to variations upon this core of Anglican identity? Is there conflict or tension between the authority given to the Bible within the Anglican tradition and that given to the episcopate? The appeal to tradition needs to be understood in a variety of ways. First, there is the appeal to patristic authority. Second, the emphasis given to the authority and nature of the Church itself and third, the particular role of the episcopate within church order. All of these have their role and place within the Anglican tradition but need careful consideration. The appeal to the patristic period is a claim that the first five centuries of the Christian tradition, in particular the ecumenical councils of the period, are normative for the Christian tradition and carry a particular weight for the Christian faith. This authority, it is claimed, is enshrined within the Anglican tradition. We need to understand the nature of this authority and how it is understood within Anglicanism. The classic work on Anglicanism, by Sykes and Booty, summarizes the claim:

> The first four ecumenical Councils of Nicaea (AD 325), Constantinople (AD 381), Ephesus (AD 431), and Chalcedon (AD 451), have a special place in Anglican theology, secondary to the Scriptures themselves, but the way in which their authority is acknowledged is complex and very important in its expression of classical Anglican theological method.[32]

The statement is interesting in a number of respects and needs to be tested. The priority of Scripture is noted. This same subordination to Scripture is also noted by Avis, but only after he has asserted that 'Anglicanism obviously recognizes the validity of the tradition of the undivided Church in supplementing and interpreting what is revealed in scripture . . .'[33] The Oxford Divines were more forthright in their assertion of patristic authority.[34]

The Articles are clear. Article 8, which follows on from the Articles dealing with Scripture, asserts the validity of the three Creeds (Nicene, Athanasian and Apostles') as proved by Scripture. Neither the patristic period *per se*, nor the first four ecumenical councils are mentioned explicitly in the Articles or other Anglican foundation documents. The Creeds, of course, emerged from this period of Christological ferment and are affirmed. However, the special place of the patristic period in Anglican theology and the importance for Anglican theological method are less clear to see. How then has this emphasis emerged? Specifically, in relation to Anglican understandings of patristic tradition, it is Lancelot Andrewes – one of the Caroline Divines – who is the key figure. Andrewes summarized authority for Anglicanism as follows:

> One canon reduced to writing by God himself, two testaments, three Creeds, four general councils, five centuries, and the series of fathers in that period – the centuries, that is, before Constantine, and two after, determine the boundary of our faith.[35]

Andrewes became a formidable theologian of the early Laudian period of Anglicanism. The overemphasis on the patristic period and the less than clear priority granted to Scripture stands ill at ease with the Anglican foundation documents. That is not to deny the relevance and importance of the patristic tradition for Christians in general or Anglicans in particular, simply to reflect upon its appropriate place not least in relation to Scripture. This patristic emphasis was picked up strongly by the Oxford Movement. The teaching of the primitive Church mediated through the Caroline era was seen by the Oxford clerics as representing the true spiritual inheritance of the Church of England. Newman appealed to the first six centuries as normative. All of this contributed to a lessening of emphasis upon the Reformation and a reaction from Evangelicals – Bishop Ryle described the church fathers as 'overrated'. With significantly more modest support for this outlook in the formularies of the Church of England, this emphasis has led scholars to ask whether the Oxford Movement was in fact engaged in a romantic rewriting of history.[36] It is easy to see the complexity of the variation in Anglican opinion, yet also important to remain clear about what belongs to the central core of belief and practice. The central historic beliefs of Anglicanism can become obscured.

Finally, in assessing the role and the claim of tradition to authority within Anglicanism, we need to consider the place of the episcopate. What is the nature of the office of bishop as understood by Anglicanism? For some the bishop represents continuity of office from the apostles, for others the bishop is the guardian of apostolic truth. Clearly these aspects are not intended to be separated. However, one emphasis gives weight to the *office* of the bishop, the other to the *teaching* of the bishop. The English Reformation settlement sought to hold these elements together in creative tension. Since that time, those who have laid claim to more Catholic interpretations of Anglicanism have tended to assert the episcopate as the *esse* (the very being) of the Church and those holding more to the Reformed tradition that it is the *bene esse* (the well being) of the Church. It would be difficult to argue that the core of Anglicanism does not have a central role for the bishop. Outside that core there have been those who have argued for different forms of oversight or have overemphasized the nature of the episcopate. A renewed epsicopate in a renewed Anglicanism, modelled on the Reformation settlement, would serve us well into the future.

None of this denied the place of human reason in theology and faith. It does, however, place any overemphasis on such rationality in perspective. The human mind is indeed a gift from God, yet since it is also susceptible to human sin, it cannot be relied upon as the ultimate source of authority. Rationality as such does not feature with any degree of significance in the Anglican approach to theology and faith in terms of ultimate authority. It is sometimes asserted that it does; the claim is a significant overstatement. Again, this is not to deny the undoubted influence of the Enlightenment and its subsequent developments upon the Anglican tradition. It is, though, to argue that as a central feature of authority it remains outside the core of the Anglican tradition.

Question and Answer – Bible, authority and the Church

What are the options for sources of authority?
The classic sources are Scripture, tradition or reason. An emphasis upon Scripture gives weight to the understanding of the Christian faith as a revealed faith. Tradition gives emphasis to the interpretative tradition, to the role of the Church, to the patristic period and the role of episcopal order and authority in the Church. Reason gives a central role to both human rational thought, especially in the light of the Enlightenment, and also to human experience, consciousness of God. Most people agree that all these factors are relevant and important. The disagreement rests upon the priority and weight attached to the different elements.

What are the key sources of authority for Anglicanism?
Scripture is the key source for Anglicanism. Its historic formularies, the Lambeth Quadrilateral, the canons and the Declaration of Assent all give to Scripture both a primacy and an authority. Tradition and reason – as expressed within the Creeds, the historic orders of ministry and the application of human rational thought, are all affirmed within Anglicanism, but only as secondary to Scripture.

I thought Anglicans believed in 'Scripture, reason and tradition'?
Well in one sense they do, but it is of significant importance to get the order and the proportionate weight attached to each correct. They are not equal. Scripture is primary.

But are we not Reformed, Catholic and liberal?
Yes and no. The catholicity of the Church (its universal apostolicity, holiness, unity) does not belong to any one tradition within the Church. The historical base of the Church lies in a clear Protestant Reformed tradition. If by liberal is meant the application of critical faculties and openness of mind and spirit to issues of the life of the Church, then a liberal spirit is part of the life of the Church. The critical point is that Catholic and liberal may represent strands of opinion but cannot and should not be used to detach the Church from its core identity and its locus of authority residing in Scripture and Scripture alone.

How important are bishops to Anglicanism?
Important rather than essential. Important as an expression of order in the life of the Church. A sign of continuity and catholicity. Provided for the well-being of the Church. The real *locus* of apostolicity lies not in the succession of bishops but in the faithful handing on of the deposit of the faith. Bishops are a useful way of ensuring and providing for this continuity but do not guarantee it. Some strands of Anglicanism have elevated the episcopate to a more central role of the very essence of the Church.

So, is the Anglican Church a confessional Church?
Yes and no. The modern penchant to deny that the Anglican Church is confessional fails to do justice to Anglican history. The Church of England is clearly confessional in that it sets out a statement of Christian and Anglican belief, in the Thirty-Nine Articles, belief that is explicated in the historic Prayer Book, canons and various declarations. This clearly associates the Church of England with the Reformed tradition which not all find palatable. The confessions of the Church of

England can, however, be distinguished from some more detailed forms of Protestant confession. Boundaries are set and a framework established, rather than second-order issues set out in detail. Anglican confessional identity does deal with particulars and not just generalities but seeks to avoid detailed prescriptions concerning church order and secondary issues. This has had the advantage of maximizing Anglican flexibility.

Why has all of this become obscured?
Three reasons. First, a loss of understanding and confidence in the historic identity of Anglicanism and how that may be applied today. Second, the impact of the Enlightenment, in reducing confidence in revelation. Third, the impact of the Oxford Movement in obscuring the Reformed heritage in both belief and practice.

Understanding Anglicanism today

A few words by way of conclusion in this historic survey of Anglican identity and history. The word complexity springs to mind! The Anglican tradition has, over the centuries, clearly been affected by a wide variety of influences. At different times and periods in its history differing weight has been attached to these emphases. We are unwise to dismiss or exclude those that give currency to particular strands of the tradition. However, it is also the case that there is a core identity of Anglicanism which lies in the Protestant Reformation settlement and the particular emphasis, understanding of Church and ministry, doctrine and practice which that embodies. Variety on both sides has indeed been part of the richness of Anglicanism, but we should be careful not to invest such variety with a weight of interpretation that it cannot bear. Similarly, caution is needed about the way in which some modern interpreters read back various aspects of the variety of Anglicanism into its core identity. When appeal is made to the pre-Reformation Church, the question must be asked, to what particular picture is appeal being made? For all of these form part of the picture of the *ecclesia anglicana*. It is also the case that readings of the Caroline Divines and the Oxford Movement can sometimes be romanticized beyond what is responsible historically or theologically. This is not a simple claim that the Anglican heritage is Reformed or Evangelical. It is certainly an assertion of the centrality and priority of the Reformation settlement. That such emphasis needs to be applied in the changing circumstances of the modern age is not doubted; but there is a great deal which has become obscured and which could usefully be made manifest once again.

Notes

1   For example, the work of Professor Grace Davie and Professor Leslie Francis.
2   Census, April 2001, Office for National Statistics.
3   Bede, *A History of the English Church and People*, (1955), London, Penguin Classics.
4   D. L. Edwards (1989), *Christian England*, London, Collins, p. 55.
5   There are numerous spellings. The convention here of 'Wyclif' is followed throughout.
6   The term 'Protestant' was first coined at the Diet of Speyer in 1529 in response to the 'protest' of the German princes against the re-imposition of Catholic authority. The term came to be used generally of those individuals and Churches which expressed the doctrinal emphases of the Reformation, either before, during or after the Reformation itself. In later centuries its usage has become more complex, not least with some elements of the Protestant tradition embracing rationalism – e.g. liberal Protestantism.
7   John Foxe's 'Book of Martyrs', officially the *Acts and Monuments of the Christian Church*, was published first in 1563 as a detailed historical description of the Reformation struggles. It is an excellent source of information, but care is needed in interpretation as it is not without polemical intent.
8   G. R. Evans (2005), *John Wyclif*, Oxford, Lion, p. 230.
9   Ibid., p. 186.
10 Ibid., pp. 9–11 and p. 243 ff.
11 Preface to The Twelve Conclusions of the Lollards, 1395, printed in A. R. Myers (ed.) (1969), *English Historical Documents, 327–1485*.
12 Ibid.
13 Martin Luther (1483–1546) was one of the early Reformers, notable for his fierce attack on the corruption of the Roman Church, especially the system of indulgences. His theological understanding revolved around the re-claiming of the idea of justification by grace through faith.
14 John Calvin (1509–1564) was the leading second-generation Reformer, based for much of his ministry in the city-state of Geneva. He had remarkable influence not least through the development of his masterpiece *The Institutes of the Christian Religion*, the final edition of which was published in 1559.

15   Cranmer was appointed Archbishop in 1532 and consecrated in 1533.

16   S. Sykes & J. Booty (eds) (1988), *The Study of Anglicanism*, London, SPCK,
     p. 3 ff.

17   D. MacCulloch (2003), 'The Church of England 1533–1603,' in S. Patten
     (ed.), *Anglicanism and the Western Christian Tradition*, Norwich, Canter-
     bury Press, and D. MacCulloch (1996), *Thomas Cranmer*, New York and
     London, Yale.

18   E. J. Bicknell (1955), *A Theological Introduction to the Thirty-Nine Articles of
     the Church of England*, London, Longmans.

19   MacCulloch, op. cit.

20   Huldrych Zwingli (1484–1531) was the early Reformer of Zurich. He
     debated with Luther throughout the 1520s on the nature of the presence
     of Christ in the Lord's Supper, taking a more explicitly Reformed
     position. Historically somewhat overshadowed by Calvin, but an import-
     ant figure and not without theological influence in the English Refor-
     mation.

21   Preface to the *Ordinal*, attached to The Book of Common Prayer, 1662.

22   The Council of Trent (1545–1563) was part of the Catholic response,
     known as the Counter-Reformation, which sought to answer key doctri-
     nal questions, to reunite the Church and to advocate renewal of Catholic
     life and faith.

23   R. Williams (2004), *Anglican Identities*, London, Darton Longman &
     Todd, p. 55.

24   Non-juror is a term used to define refusal to swear an oath of allegiance
     to a monarch. Such oaths have featured on several occasions in Anglican
     history and have always generated dissent (non-juring) from various
     directions.

25   Richard Baxter (1615–1691) was Vicar of Kidderminster from 1647 to
     1661, the author of many works of Puritan spirituality. He was widely
     respected for his ministry both in Kidderminster and elsewhere.

26   P. Nockles (2003), 'Survivals or new arrivals? The Oxford Movement and
     the nineteenth-century construction of Anglicanism', in Patten, op. cit.,
     pp. 146–7.

27   *Tracts for the Times* (1833–1841), Tract 90, Introduction, Oxford.

28   Sykes & Booty, op. cit., p. xi.

29   C. R. Seitz (2001), *Figured Out*, Louisville, Westminster John Knox Press,
     p. 60.

30   C. Podmore (2005), *Aspects of Anglican Identity*, London, CHP, pp. 42–57.

31   Ibid., p. 57.

32   Sykes & Booty, op. cit., p. 189.

33   P. Avis (2000), *The Anglican Understanding of the Church*, London , SPCK,
     p. 51.

34   P. Nockles (2003), op. cit., pp. 148–9.

35   Sykes & Booty, op. cit., p. 237.

36   Nockles, op., cit., p. 148.

2

Understanding Evangelical identity

The quest for identity

'I knew what constituted an Evangelical in former times. I have no clear notion what constitutes one now.'[1] So said the Earl of Shaftesbury towards the end of his life. Anglicanism is not one monolithic whole. Exactly the same is the case when considering the Evangelical tradition. Evangelical is a convenient description which gathers together a wide range of theological and spiritual persuasions. Indeed, some of these understandings appear to be in tension, if not conflict, with each other. The question is whether there is a distinguishable core to the identity of the Evangelical tradition and what variation there may be around that centre. Identity is central to purpose. Similarly a spiritual tradition which loses sight of its roots and foundations and fails to pass on a deep understanding of that tradition is doomed to failure. The pressures will come in different ways. Some will seek to broaden the definition so much that there is little or no substance to the heart of its identity while others will enshrine secondary matters as part of the nucleus.

The rising prominence of Evangelicals

These questions of identity and purpose are important for two main reasons. First, Evangelicals form part of a significant spiritual tradition within Christianity with its roots in the Reformation. Evangelicalism reflects, at least in part, key Reformation principles; especially *sola scriptura* (by Scripture alone) and *sola fide* (by faith alone). The way in which Evangelicalism has interacted with wider intellectual trends has also been a recurring theme of studies of Evangelicalism as the movement emerged in its fullness in the eighteenth and nineteenth centuries. Thus Evangelicalism has been shaped by the prevailing philosophical climate, especially the Enlightenment, but also by the later intellectual course of Romanticism. However, a proper study of the phenomenon of Evangelicalism must also engage with the fact that the movement influenced, affected and shaped society itself.

Second, the modern growth and strength of the Evangelical tradition both within and beyond the Anglican Church is an important factor. Measurement is difficult but both the perception and the accumulation of evidence at least suggest that Evangelicals feature increasingly significantly in the life of the Church. The growth in membership of the Evangelical Alliance and the work of Peter Brierley on English church attendance are both signs of Evangelical growth and vitality.[2] Partly at least this is because of decline in other Christian traditions, so Evangelicalism itself may have grown only moderately, or declined less fast than other traditions. Similarly the Christian Research Association has shown that Evangelical churches provide a disproportionate amount of the income of the Church. Within the Church of England in excess of 70 per cent of the ordinands training in residential colleges are at the six Evangelical colleges (the same six colleges together trained only 36 per cent of serving diocesan bishops, 37 per cent of suffragans, 21 per cent of deans and 31 per cent of archdeacons), though of course this masks a shift away from residential training. On the General Synod the Evangelical group in recent years have held around 50 per cent of the votes in the House of Laity, 30 per cent in the House of Clergy and 10 per cent in the House of Bishops. In the newly elected General Synod of 2005, Evangelicals were elected as Prolocutor of the Convocation of Canterbury (the Chairman of the House of Clergy for Province of Canterbury), Chairman and Vice-Chairman of the House of Laity.

Clearly, the realities of life, politics, theology and ecclesiastical interests combine to make the reality significantly less neat than the crude statistics might suggest. However, when combined with the recent historical perspective of both the Puritan revival in the Church of England in the postwar years and the Charismatic revival from the 1960s onwards, the continued importance of Evangelicalism as both a movement and a phenomenon is clear to see. In the modern Church, mega churches such as Holy Trinity Brompton, wider Charismatic movements such as New Wine and Soul Survivor, church planting, Alpha and other initiatives are very significant indeed alongside more traditional examples of Evangelical witness and piety, both within and beyond the Anglican Church.

Evangelicalism in North America is a complex phenomenon. Within a culture that is, on the face of it at least, more explicitly Christian (notwithstanding the separation of Church and state enshrined in the American constitution), Evangelicalism is dominant. Sometimes this is expressed through the strength of a particular denomination (e.g. the Southern Baptists) and on other occasions through para-church organisations such as Focus on the Family. The political impact of Evangelicals in the USA has been very significant indeed, at least in some respects. Contrary to the situation in England, Evangelicals in the Episcopal Church seem to be an oppressed minority. However, they have continued to have meaningful influence in a number of dioceses and through international networks.

Beginnings

When did Evangelicalism begin and how did the movement develop? The term derives from the Revival in eighteenth-century England, usually associated with the conversion of John Wesley in 1738 – in a way that historians rather love by linking a movement or trend with a particular event. The reality was more complex, though the impact no less important. The Revival in England spread quickly both within and without the established Church. The history has been well described elsewhere.[3] Opponents of Evangelicalism used the term 'enthusiasts', and Evangelicals had to battle for ordination, for livings and for wider acceptance. In essence, there had been a spiritual quickening of heart and soul. Orthodox Christian belief became not an intellectual exercise but rather a discernment of God's very word (in the Bible) into spiritual life and action in the heart of the believer. As such it crossed continents as well as denominations. It emboldened individuals to action both as individuals and corporately in Evangelical societies. The movement brought new life to established Churches and carried with it an urgency that had particular cogency on the edge – the frontiers of industrial England, of the North American colonies and of unexplored Africa. Very quickly the movement became transnational as well as trans-denominational.

In England the factors contributing to the Revival have been set out as a combination of Puritan theology, High Church orthodoxy and a reaction against Enlightenment rationalism.[4] Perhaps more positively it was the influence of Pietism, a strand of belief with traces back into aspects of the more radical elements of the Reformation (and hence the ones least attractive to ecclesiastical establishments) that combined with Reformed doctrine to bring about a new force in Protestantism. It was a new era, a renewed popular Protestantism. This force grew rapidly. The charitable assumption of Tudor England that both the nation and its citizens were, by definition, Christian, was already being exploded by the advance of Enlightenment rationalism. Although scholars have sought to reclaim the religious history of the eighteenth century,[5] there was at least a quietism, if not a degree of spiritual deadness. Certainly spiritual dryness (perhaps imparted by the rationalism of the Enlightenment) was seen on both sides of the Atlantic as part of the setting into which revival came. New birth was needed. The gospel was to be proclaimed. So, the gospel message was indeed set forth – in the open air, to the miners of Kingswood, in the conversion of clergy, including one by his own sermon,[6] in hymnody, in missionary endeavour at home and overseas. A spiritual awakening.

Across the Atlantic similar currents were at work in parallel. There had been contact between Wesley and the colonies before Wesley's conversion. Jonathan Edwards had a conversion experience in 1727, some 11 years before Wesley's Aldersgate Street 'warming of the heart'. The old Puritan faith was ripe for revival, again, not least in partial response to increasing rationalism. In 1734, revival broke out in the county of Northampton, Massachusetts, under Jonathan Edwards about which he later wrote *A Faithful Narrative of the Surprising Work of God*. By the early 1740s Whitefield and Wesley were visiting the New World with powerful impact; printing and publishing as well as personal contact were spreading news of revival on both sides of the Atlantic. A new Reformation. John Wesley (1703–1791) and George Whitefield (1714–1770) were both key figures in the Revival on both sides of the Atlantic. They clashed over the extent of redemption (see page 66).

The effect of the Revival on Anglicanism is of particular significance. In both England and North America revival took place both within and without the established Church. The history of both the Church of England and, indeed, of England itself, would be incomplete without recognition of the extent of the influence of the Revival on the established Church. By the mid-nineteenth century Evangelicals within the established Church were a powerful force, with mission societies at home and overseas, with bishops in post, livings built up and protected by the patronage system, and with faithful pastoral ministries being established and developed. In addition to all of that, prominent political leaders motivated by Evangelical Christian faith influenced the transformation of society. This is not to gloss over complexities and difficulties from the theological to the political, but it is to emphasize both the significance of Evangelicalism and its clear location within the Church of England.

Factors in North America were less straightforward. The early revivalists were Calvinist ministers like Cotton Mather and Jonathan Edwards, outside the established Church. However, the visits of Wesley and Whitefield were from ministers of the established Church in England and they sought to reach these same ministers in the Americas, though with more limited success. Whitefield was challenged due to his description of the Presbyterian Gilbert Tennant as a faithful minister in Christ, by his and Wesley's openness to working with non-Anglicans and by his willingness to allow a Baptist minister to lead a Communion service and even to receive Communion from his hands.[7] However, elsewhere in America, both before and after independence, Evangelicals did make progress in the established Church, mainly in the more low church areas of the middle and southern states. Examples included Deveraux Jarrett in Virginia, Alexander Griswold and Richard Moore. Indeed Evangelicals continued to have significant influence in the Episcopal Church until being eclipsed by a combination of Oxford Movement influence and the religious pluralism of the Protestant denominations; there were many to choose from with their roots in America rather than England.

A significant factor was the departure of eight clergy and 20 laity in 1873 to form the Reformed Episcopal Church. The reasons were concern over excessive ritualism (influence of Oxford Movement), an exclusiveness of the Episcopal Church which denied the essential doctrinal catholicity of Evangelicals, and, in short, the loss of Protestant witness within Episcopalianism. The Reformed Episcopal Church set out Scripture as the highest authority, adherence to the plain meaning of the Thirty-Nine Articles and worship centred on the Book of Common Prayer. The Revd W. R. Nicholson set out his reasons for joining the Reformed Episcopal Church as the impact of Romanism, the presumption of baptismal regeneration, the exclusivism of the Episcopal Church, priesthood, ritualism and teaching on the real presence.[8] The impact of the formation of the Reformed Episcopal Church is important. Evangelicals were already weaker in ECUSA than in the Church of England. Similarly, although there were departures from the Church of England over time, they were small and few, though often also over baptismal regeneration.[9] In this the Gorham Judgment was of huge significance. To that we will return in the next chapter.

In the USA the departure of many Evangelicals weakened the witness even further. It is, however, significant that, as in so many of these divisions, there were many Protestant and orthodox clergy who remained within ECUSA. That tradition, although reduced in size and influence, has continued with both the Morning Prayer tradition of worship, and a clear Protestant doctrinal understanding of the Articles, Prayer Book and of the whole basis of the Protestant Episcopal Church of the USA. Indeed the Reformed Episcopal Church itself remained a small denomination. We will return in the next chapter to look at both the impact and the consequences of all of this on the current-day dominance of liberal theology within ECUSA, not least in matters of human sexuality.

So in the outbreak of revival we see some common factors. Revival built upon the tradition of the Reformation on both sides of the Atlantic. It reacted against formalism, rationalism and dryness, and the Revival sought a spiritual awakening to new life in Christ. Transnational influences were significant factors, for Evangelicalism was, and is, a worldwide movement. Nevertheless, the way in which Evangelicalism expressed itself was affected by local conditions and circumstances, and not everything can be understood by unitary themes.

Identity

There were also antecedents both theologically and spiritually. The most significant precursor was the Reformation. The term Evangelical has been used positively and negatively both at the time of the Reformation (very occasionally) and in scholarly study since (more often, for example, MacCulloch). Hence there is a connection to the Reformation and the theology of the Reformation but its nature and manner require careful investigation for the link is not an exact one. The fact that the Reformation itself is a term that embraces a wide range of theological and spiritual traditions is an additional element in recognizing not just the diversity of its identity but also its complexity.

Thus the development and use of the term Evangelical, rather like its relative, Protestant, is not straightforward. In medieval times the word was used to describe the New Testament itself, its message, or that of a particular gospel. The term was in use in some of the writings of the continental Reformation in the 1520s, and was adopted by Luther to contrast the biblical way of salvation over and against the corruption of the Catholic Church. Following the second Diet of Speyer in 1529 when six princes and 14 German cities protested against the revocation of the religious liberties guaranteed three years earlier, the term Protestant came into more general usage. In modern German usage the word Evangelical simply aligns the term with the state or national institutional Protestant Churches. More recently it has come to be used by scholars to describe those committed to the evangel and the Scriptures in England during the course of the English Reformation prior to the more general usage of Protestant from the reign of Mary Tudor (1553–1558). However, that is largely to replace one anachronism with another, given that Evangelical has come to have particular meaning. The terminology is now most generally used, both by scholars and in more popular religion, to describe the popular religious movement grounded in the Protestant Reformation but enlivened by the spiritual renewal of Pietism, that came to express itself in the Evangelical Revival and the Great Awakening; a renewed and revived English-speaking Protestantism.

The question of definition: what is an Evangelical?

What is an Evangelical? We have drawn together the building blocks of Evangelical identity, but the question of definition is of particular importance for both Evangelical self-understanding and the exploration of Evangelical interaction with other traditions, not least Anglicanism. Given that we have already noted that Evangelicalism cannot be understood as a single whole, but is rather a somewhat complex mosaic of beliefs, influences and practices, then it is important, first of all, to distinguish between methodological approaches to the matter of definition.

Generalist

The understanding that has gained the most currency is the *generalist* method. This has been pioneered in the modern era by David Bebbington in his seminal work on the history of Evangelicalism.[10] Its great strength lies in the inclusivity of the range and breadth of Evangelical belief and in relating Evangelicalism to the philosophical and intellectual movements which have emerged since the Enlightenment. In essence this approach isolated four key characteristics of Evangelicalism. The aim was to find a framework which could embrace and explain the essential characteristics of all those who historically had laid claim to the label of 'Evangelical'. Bebbington developed a 'quadrilateral of priorities', conversionism, activism, biblicism and crucicentrism.[11]

The need for conversion, for new birth, has always been central to Evangelical belief. This was amply demonstrated at the time of the Revival with the high-profile conversion stories of Wesley and later of John Newton, the former captain of a slave trader, and the spiritual priority given to 'the story of conversion'. It was also shown in expectations of conversion in the pastoral ministry, including the story of William Haslam, the clergyman already noted as converted by his own sermon in 1851. Conversion was a central act of grace in the life and heart of the sinner – the point of conversion was frequently one of crisis. Thus preaching for conversion, expectation of conversion and desire for conversion were central features of the Revival. Such desire was expressed with such intensity that it was often accompanied by scenes of deep emotional stirrings as the convicted sinner came under the saving grace of the gospel.

Activism is another characteristic of Bebbington's generalist approach. Conversion changed lives. The new believer was expected to be active in a number of ways. Three particular activities were (a) changing their own moral lifestyle (b) changing the moral lifestyle of others and (c) spreading the faith. Evangelical ministry thus came to be characterized by earnestness and seriousness. In an age when the norms of clerical life were often those of simony (the selling of livings), pluralism (clergy holding numerous posts to the neglect of most) and non-residence (holding a post in one place, but residing in another), Evangelical clergy quickly became identified as those who were untiring in parish duties and indefatigable in their commitment. Social welfare missions were also the beneficiaries of this Evangelical activism, especially under the influence of Lord Shaftesbury and after repeated visits to England of revivalist preachers such as D. L. Moody.

The third of Bebbington's quadrilateral in this generalist approach is biblicism, devotion to the content and place of Holy Scripture. This has been reflected within the Evangelical tradition by the development of ideas of inspiration, authority and spiritual power. The Bible is the inspired Word of God, though for the generalist the nature of the inspiration remains a secondary matter to the fact of inspiration. Since the Bible is inspired by God then it carries the authority of God. The Scriptures thus, in continuity with the Reformation, are for the Evangelical the final and indeed only authority in matters of both faith and practice for the Christian. The spiritual power of the living word is exemplified by the central place of the sermon.

Fourth, Bebbington considers what he termed crucicentrism to describe the central place in Evangelical belief of the death of Jesus. The cross is the place of reconciliation and forgiveness. Bebbington describes 'a cloud of witnesses'[12] and the doctrine also defined Evangelicals over and against Anglo-Catholicism in the nineteenth century. Jesus was born in order to die. Although Bebbington notes that Christ's death in our place as substitute was the normal Evangelical belief, it was not universal and lessened over the course of the nineteenth century especially in Methodism. There was also some disagreement over what we might see as a rather esoteric debate of 'for whom did Christ die', for everybody (the Arminian position) or just for the elect (the Calvinist understanding). Most Evangelicals were moderate Calvinists; the salvation of the cross was preached to all; it was the elect who would respond. However, above all distinctions, nuances of belief and other disagreements, Evangelicals were united about the centrality of the cross.

Propositional

A criticism that can be offered of the generalist approach to definition is just that; it is generalist. By placing the emphasis on breadth and inclusivity, one of the most historically enduring characteristics of Evangelicalism is lost – that it is marked out by the specifics of belief. Theological conviction has always been a central tenet of Evangelical expression and belief. However, the matter is more complex when we open up the debate of which doctrines or which aspects of doctrinal conviction are central to Evangelicalism. An example of a more specifically doctrinal approach to the question of identity can be seen in a series of addresses given by the prominent postwar nonconformist Evangelical, Dr Martyn Lloyd-Jones, to the International Fellowship of Evangelical Students in 1971. These talks were reprinted in 1992 under the title *What is an Evangelical?* The features mentioned by Bebbington were all there: the centrality of Scripture, evangelism, the need for new birth and the cross. However, the description was expanded to include within the defining characteristics of an Evangelical, opposition to ecumenism, the doctrine of the Church, the centrality of preaching, doctrinal certainty, distrust of reason, a low view of the sacraments and creation over evolution. If the problem with the generalist approach is the wider the definition the less the precision, then the difficulty with the propositional approach is the greater the precision, the narrower the definition.

Some, and this has had appeal to Anglican Evangelicals, have sought a middle way between the more inclusive and exclusivist approaches, set out by James Packer and then reasserted by Alister McGrath.[13] Packer offers six Evangelical distinctives: the supremacy of Holy Scripture, the majesty of Jesus Christ, the Lordship of the Holy Spirit, the necessity of conversion, the priority of evangelism and the importance of fellowship. Laudable though this attempt is, and with much insight – Packer and McGrath do link their descriptive material to doctrinal emphasis on justification and atonement – to what extent these particular six factors can be seen as determinative of Evangelical identity is not entirely clear.

Sociological

A third approach to definition has been to adopt a sociological perspective. This understanding is based around the assertion that definition flows from belonging and identification. At its more popular level it is expressed by association with key structures – traditionally Evangelicals have linked together in common cause through organizations such as the Church Missionary Society (CMS), now known as the Church Mission Society. Indeed historically there is some support for this approach. In the ferment of the Evangelicalism that was the 1820s (see pages 82–86), the British and Foreign Bible Society (the Bible Society), and, in the 1920s, CMS endured doctrinal divisions within the membership. Although alternative societies were formed (the Trinitarian Bible Society and the Bible Churchmen's Missionary Society (BCMS) respectively) the power of the hold of the parent societies was so strong that there were 'conservative' activists in both cases who stayed with the parent societies and in some cases supported both.[14] However, being formed in a tradition and identifying with a particular expression of Christianity is unlikely to be sustained as any meaningful concept if it is reduced to membership of, participation in or identity with one or other pre-determined organization or structure.

David Wells adopted a more nuanced version of this approach by developing three centres or streams around which Evangelicals congregate: a confessional stream, a trans-confessional strand and a Charismatic grouping.[15] The first group would be essentially propositional. The second draws on transatlantic understandings of the nature of Evangelicalism as crossing boundaries of culture, continent and denomination. The third epicentre is that of Charismatic experience, a point of unity which can transcend all boundaries, but *in extremis* can also transcend doctrinal belief. The description is helpful and insightful. The problem is in the tension between the differing elements. Is Evangelical unity based upon a common life or a common faith?

A new framework: four spiritual marks

The problem of definition is that of boundaries. Different assessments will offer differing prescriptions as to what lies within and without the boundaries of definition. The more generalist the approach, the more inclusive, but this may lead to the specifics of belief being subsumed within the overall description, thus masking important differences and emphases. However, the nature of Evangelical identity extends deeper than a series of statements of belief. The spiritual disposition of an Evangelical encompasses much more than either general description or precise doctrinal formulations. What these descriptive approaches miss is the spiritual heart of the tradition.

There are four centres to Evangelical spiritual identity: authority, doctrine, spirituality and transformation.[16] These distinctives together form the heart of Evangelical identity. These centres of identity operate like the four chambers of the heart, the seat of the emotions and the essential pumping mechanism to give life. These emphases combine a theological understanding based upon divine revelation, a confessional belief, spiritual experience and transforming action.

First, then, authority. The Bible always features in questions of Evangelical identity. The issue, however, is not just of the Bible's *centrality* but also of its *authority*. Evangelicalism is based upon the belief that Christianity is a revealed faith and that the revelation took place certainly in the person of Jesus, but more particularly in the Holy Scriptures, the Word of God. Hence the Bible is not just important but it is the final authority in all matters of faith, belief and practice. It is from this premise that the importance of preaching flows. Evangelicals are not the only Christian tradition to hold a high view of the Bible, but it is the authority with which it is invested that marks out the Evangelical tradition. However, for Evangelicals the Bible is not only authoritative but it also carries with it a clarity of message and purpose. The word used to describe this is perspicuity. Essential to Evangelical belief is not only the revelation of Scripture and its authority, but that it contains a clear message, accessible to all – the good news of the gospel.

The second centre is the doctrinal heart of the faith. Generalists tend to avoid it, propositionalists have nothing else to say. However, the specifics of Evangelical belief cannot be simply reduced to the centrality of the cross – a feature of Western Christianity generally. The distinguishing mark of an Evangelical is the particular understanding of the cross. It is perhaps here that

Evangelicalism owes most to the Puritan heritage with an emphasis on sin, the substitutionary atonement and justification by faith. Evangelicalism is salvationist. It is not universalist. If conversion is to have any meaning then conversion had to be from one thing to another. To what was a person converted? The understanding of the atoning sacrifice of Jesus Christ upon the cross was for the first 150 years of the movement universally accepted as both substitutionary and penal. There were, of course, unhelpful disputes about related matters of free will, but those who departed from the substitutionary understanding of the atonement were seen as departing from the Evangelical faith.

Third, then, spirituality. What are the spiritual marks of an Evangelical? That is not to separate spirituality from doctrine but to ask how an Evangelical understands the relationship of the believer to Jesus Christ. The inadequacy of a simply propositional approach is that such an analysis struggles to move beyond the doctrinal statements to matters of spiritual relationship. Evangelicals are converted people, converted to new belief, but they have also received new birth into a new familial relationship with God as Father, Son and Holy Spirit. The spiritual mark of the Evangelical is that the relationship with God is marked out as a personal relationship with the Saviour. It is a relationship of intimacy, love and obedience. It is marked by prayer, that itself is personal and intimate and, above all else, expectant. The personal Saviour answers prayer.

Finally, transformation. The Evangelical is marked by a passion for and a sense of urgency in the priority of the gospel. The gospel is not just something to be believed; it is to be lived and acted upon. The transformation is both individual and corporate. Life has changed. Alongside the new birth comes a sense of accountability, a recognition of the judgement of God, the return of Christ one day to earth and the commands of Scripture to spread the gospel to all nations. Passion and urgency are further spiritual marks of an Evangelical that illustrate the transformation that has been received and is to be shared. Evangelism is central. However, transformation for the Evangelical has corporate implications for society as well as individual (see Chapter 4). Certainly there have been tensions within Evangelicalism over the relative roles of evangelism and social action, but historically the transformation which has marked out Evangelicals has been both an individual one and one for society at large (in other words, as noted earlier, Evangelicalism has in some significant ways shaped society itself).

Evangelical distinctives

The spiritual marks of an Evangelical have been set out as the four centres of authority, doctrine, spirituality and transformation. This core is based around the authority and clarity of Scripture, the substitutionary atonement of Christ, the personal relationship with Jesus and the transformation of both individual and society. To understand the Evangelical tradition more fully, in all its complexity, we need to consider these distinctive features in more depth.

Bible

If the Bible marks out for Evangelicals the authoritative and clear revelation of God, how then exactly does the Evangelical tradition understand the nature of Scripture? In the early years of the Evangelical movement, a group of prominent Evangelicals began to meet to discuss matters of faith and belief. The group was formed in 1783 by John Newton, Richard Cecil, Henry Foster and Eli Bates, the first three ordained, the latter a layman. They were joined over time by others. They were mainly from the established Church of England, but there were some dissenters who were members. There were also country members who attended from time to time, including Charles Simeon of Cambridge. They met at St John's, Bedford Row, they named themselves The Eclectic Society and we have the notes of the theological discussions made available at the time by The Revd Josiah Pratt, for 21 years the Secretary of CMS. These notes are an excellent source for the nature of theological belief among early Evangelicals.[17]

These early leaders had a number of discussions concerning the Bible. On 19 January 1800 the Society debated the nature of the inspiration of the Scriptures. John Venn, Rector of Clapham, asserted two aspects of inspiration. First, plenary inspiration where the particular words were chosen and inspired by God, not by the individual as, for example, in much of Old Testament prophecy. Second, superintendent inspiration where, in writing plain facts of history the writer is under the general inspiration of

God but uses his own style. Venn asked about the nature of the Holy Spirit's superintendence over the words of the apostles. Henry Foster responded that 'the writers were influenced not only as to *matter*, but as to *words*'.[18] John Newton maintained that 'when St Paul says he speaks by *permission*, he implies that on all other occasions it is by *direction*'.[19] We see here very early on the setting down of a clear understanding of the verbal and plenary inspiration of Holy Scripture. However, in the same meeting, nuances can be noted. Richard Cecil advocated a more general superintendence, 'in writing a transaction, there needs no more than a care over the writer, to prevent his uttering anything which is not truth'.[20] This was reinforced by Thomas Scott, the noted biblical commentator:

> It is an astonishing truth, and an irrefragable evidence of divine inspiration, that shepherds and kings and men of such various characters should write a book agreeing in all its parts.[21]

So here we see inspiration asserted as a negative protection against error. There was unity upon the fact of inspiration, and some variety over its particular nature.

With the rise of the Tractarians in the 1830s, conflict over the understanding of Scripture hardened. Partly this was due to Evangelical concern that the rising Oxford Movement was asserting the equivalence of tradition alongside Scripture. The actual statements of the Tractarians were, of course, carefully nuanced. In his *The Rule of Faith* (1838), Henry Manning claimed that in matters of interpretation the most reliable witness was the universal agreement of the early Church. The Tractarians, through Isaac Williams, also gave weight to the mystical interpretation of the Scriptures. All of this sat ill at ease with the Eclectic understanding expressed by Thomas Scott that, 'the clear passages are to explain the obscure and not the obscure the clear'.[22]

A variety of Evangelical writers responded to the Tractarians.[23] William Goode delivered the masterpiece in *The Divine Rule of Faith and Practice*, first published in 1842. Goode maintained that the Scripture alone was canonical, the supreme and sole Word of God, authoritative, sufficient and complete. Evangelicals denied revelation outside of Holy Scripture. Toon quotes Goode:

And if Holy Scripture is thus the sole infallible and authoritative Rule of faith, it follows, of course, that it is to its decision alone that we must appeal, as of absolute authority and infallible, in *controversies concerning the faith*; and hence it is justly called the sole infallible *Judge of controversies of faith*, as being that which alone gives an infallible testimony on the subject.[24]

Scripture alone. Sufficient and final. Earlier debate over the means of inspiration was seen as a luxury which could not be afforded when the Tractarians were perceived to be elevating tradition as the final interpreter as Scripture. It was a challenge to the sufficiency of Scripture and could not go unmet.

At the National Evangelical Anglican Congress in 2003, David Peterson, the Principal of Oak Hill Theological College, re-asserted this basic understanding of the nature of the Bible for Evangelicals:

Orthodox Christians have traditionally affirmed the perfection of Scripture in terms of its *infallibility*, its *supreme authority* and its *sufficiency* for bringing people to a saving knowledge of God.[25]

Not all welcome this maintenance of the traditional understanding of Scripture. The impact of Enlightenment rationality and development of literary critical methods of biblical interpretation have made some feel uneasy. Similarly, it is argued by those who analyse our culture that in this post-modern world there is no such thing as an absolute truth, simply different truths competing with each other.

If the idea of scriptural authority is generally accepted among Evangelicals, then that of its infallibility or inerrancy is certainly not. There are two observations to make regarding infallibility. First, an *a priori* understanding that, given the agreed nature of Christianity as a revealed faith, and the agreed character and nature of God, it is a reasonable position to maintain that the Lord's revelation would be reliable (as well as complete). Second, some caution is needed in what is meant by infallibility or inerrancy. The Evangelical position which has developed is that infallibility applies to Scripture (a) as originally given and (b) as correctly interpreted. We do not possess the original autographs. However, we trust God in his character for the reliability of his provision in divine revelation. This, however, means that we are dealing with manuscript copies of the Scriptures. This should encourage Evangelical biblical scholarship in the hermeneutical task of interpretation, but with the conviction that God has clearly spoken in his Word and is entirely trustworthy. However, it also means that the Evangelical faith is not overthrown by minor issues deriving from copyists' errors (inconsistency between manuscripts). All of this with a humility that it is God's revealed Word that is being handled. As John Stott has said:

> For Evangelicals emphatically do not claim inerrancy either for a faulty text or for every weird and wonderful interpretation . . .[26]

As regards the sufficiency of Scripture, the testimony is of Christ himself. Christ is the incarnate Word, for whom Scripture at all points was sufficient for his needs and who demonstrated in his life complete and utter reliance upon the Old Testament Scriptures. What was good enough for Jesus is good enough also for today's Evangelicals. To this testimony is then added that of Scripture itself, in the New Testament, in 2 Timothy 3.15–17 that all Scripture is God-breathed. The inadequacy of any alternative, whether tradition, reason or experience, is illustrated by God's own character. Human sin means that only divine revelation is sufficient. We should, of course, expect nothing less from God. Indeed, it is from Scripture that all other doctrinal emphases flow.

The cross

The cross is an accepted part of the defining characteristics of an Evangelical. In fact, it is a particular doctrinal understanding of the cross which marks out Evangelical witness and identity. The emphasis is on Jesus Christ taking our place on the cross (substitution) and bearing the sin, penalty and due wrath of the Father (penal). This central feature of the Evangelical tradition reaches right back into the Reformed heritage of the movement. It has remained a constant belief, although it has been challenged both from within and without the movement. It is the power of this understanding of the cross that for the Evangelical makes the grace of God and the forgiveness and reconciliation of the cross effective in the personal lives of believers. In other words the distinctive Evangelical doctrine of the atonement is significantly more than an example, or even representative. It is personal and transformational. Evangelical doctrine is broad enough to encompass a range of understandings of the atonement. However, any theory which evacuates the cross of the substitutionary nature of the atonement and the consequences, positive and negative, of the penalty that is borne, also evacuates the Christian faith of central purpose and meaning.

Martin Luther's great 're-discovery' was of the understanding of the righteousness of God, as being not something that humanity worked towards, but an essential characteristic of God, which was imputed to us through faith. We were declared righteous before the righteous God on the basis of the grace of God through faith ('justification by faith'). God's grace was a free gift, and undeserved. This was part of the wonder of the salvation brought about for us in Jesus. For Luther, justification was achieved through the cross. That was where atonement took place, how God revealed himself, not least in the hiddenness, pain and suffering of the cross.

Calvin, in his *Institutes of the Christian Religion*, formulated the concept with his characteristic clarity. According to Calvin 'when Christ is hanged upon the cross, he makes himself subject to the curse'.[27] This penalty was due to us on account of our sin and through the cross was lifted from us and transferred to Christ. So Christ acquired all our sin and impurity and we were clothed with his purity. He discharged all satisfaction through his sacrifice, turning aside God's wrath. So as the Evangelical tradition developed, the atonement continued to be emphasized, partly in distinction from other traditions that gave weight to the incarnation. Certainly questions were raised during the formative period of Evangelical development, not least over the extent of the atonement – did Christ die only for the elect (Whitefield, following Calvin) or was the offer of salvation universal (Wesley)? Much ink was spilt and there was much misunderstanding. However, questions were also raised by these early Evangelicals as to the manner of Christ's death – as substitute or representative – and whether the sacrificial death of Jesus was to be described in penal terms.

The Eclectic Evangelicals were united in believing that Christ died for our sins as a substitute. Thus John Clayton said at a meeting of The Eclectic Society that the sin of a believer was imputed to Christ as a substitute or surety[28] and Henry Foster, on another occasion, that the substitution of Christ for sinners was the greatest possible act of love to his children.[29] Thus Christ took our sins and Christ's righteousness was imputed to us on the basis of faith – justification by faith. The Evangelical understanding of the cross was linked to the doctrine of assurance which gave a very personal and individual assurance of the certainty of the forgiveness of sins; hence also the personal and specific nature of the understanding of the cross. However, these early Evangelicals also provided cogent theological reasoning as to why the atonement was effective. It was because as our substitute Jesus bore the penalty of death which was rightly due to us that the atonement was the ground of hope. Hence the substitution was penal, summarized at The Eclectic Society by Josiah Pratt:

> Then we must represent Christ to them as a SURETY, as a SUB-STITUTE, and his ability and willingness to discharge their debt *for* them; that he *atones* for their crimes; and that he works out *another righteousness for them.* This is a most essential branch of his mediatorial excellence. It is the ground of all our hopes. What he *did* and *suffered*, he did and suffered in all our *stead.*[30]

The self-consistency of Evangelical belief depended upon an effective dealing with the wrath of God discernible in the Scriptures.

In the mid-nineteenth century Evangelicals affirmed their understanding of the centrality of the atonement against the idea of 'reserve' advanced by the Tractarians. This was the idea that the essentially mysterious doctrine of the atonement should be taught only gradually, albeit profoundly, as the baptized lived out their Christian lives in increasing obedience to God. The Oxford clerics recoiled at the weight given to the atonement by Evangelicals. It was not that they denied its importance, rather that they emphasized its mystery rather than its clarity. Reinforced by concerns over Newman's understanding of justification, Evangelicals asserted the centrality of the doctrine of the atonement. This understanding of the atonement was not without critics. This was partially fuelled by Wesleyan emphasis on the universality of the offer of salvation, the rise of a more liberal Evangelicalism in the early twentieth century and among some contemporary Evangelicals today. This debate is discussed in the excursus on page 72.

The notion of the atonement as substitutionary and penal has been a controlling model of the cross for Evangelicals. It draws strongly for its scriptural authority on passages such as Isaiah 53.6–10, Romans 3.25, 2 Corinthians 5.21, Galatians 3.13, Hebrews 9.11–10.22 and 1 Peter 3.18. The emphasis on substitution, penalty and propitiatory sacrifice all link strongly with Evangelical concern for assurance, individual forgiveness and redemption exemplified in the cross. Without the cross there is no Christianity. Without the biblical emphasis on the particular nature of what is achieved on the cross by way of substitution and satisfaction, the cross is left devoid of all meaning.

Christ

Jesus Christ is the spiritual centre of Evangelicalism. Essentially this is because it is Christ who forgives (through his work on the cross), but it is also because it is *to* Christ and *for* Christ that the sinner is converted. The relationship to Christ for the Evangelical is a personal one, involving individual submission, obedience, worship and discipleship. The relationship is marked by prayer. The majesty of Jesus Christ towers over everything and everyone else for the Evangelical. For the Evangelical, discipleship involves obedience to Christ and to God's Word in the Scriptures. It is marked by both commitment and intensity. It is exemplified by personal calling. It is shown in a submission to divine providence.

Divine providence

Evangelicals have an acute sense of divine providence, that is the direct intervention of God in the personal life of the believer. Firstly, this is expressed in call, which is both general and specific. In a more general sense the call is to faithful personal discipleship of Jesus Christ. For the Evangelical call will always have a significant personal element. Call is not only to be responded to, but to be obeyed. This has been expressed throughout Evangelical history by the call to serve the Lord in pioneer situations, either overseas or in unfruitful settings in industrial England or, quite simply, in everyday parish situations. The call is a command for the Evangelical. It cannot be set aside. It is inextricably linked to the call to evangelism and to faithfulness to the apostolic gospel.

Examples include the call of Hudson Taylor to China and of the Cambridge Seven in similar vein. It includes the call of city missionaries in nineteenth-century London. It includes the call to ordination and the call to civic service in politics and elsewhere in society. The call is for clergy and laity alike, recognizing the heritage of the priesthood of all believers. Evangelicals recognize the corporate nature of call – the call of God is to be affirmed by the Church – but the emphasis is placed upon the individual. The call may come at any time and in numerous ways. This would include the deathbed (there are many examples of deathbed conversions in Evangelicalism) and, most usually, through the preaching of the Word of God.

Providence is concerned with the nature of God's action in the world and for the Evangelical extends into the everyday life of the Christian disciple. God has not retired to his armchair to direct affairs from a distance; rather he is intimately involved in every detail of every day in the life of the believer. The distinction has usually been drawn between general providence (God's overall working through the order of the world) – an understanding common to the majority of Christians – and special providence, 'an effect produced by the appointment of God',[31] (in other words, God working directly). The early Evangelicals displayed considerable reserve in assigning events to special providence, reflecting the influence of Calvinist determinism. Nevertheless, the person of Napoleon Bonaparte, lotteries, fast days and cholera were all seen as examples of special providence, often reflecting the judgement of God upon sin in the nation.[32] As time went on, with the impact of premillennialism within the Evangelical tradition, the notion of an interventionist God became even more prominent. With the associated emergence of faith missions, the idea of providence operating in the everyday life of the believer (not least in terms of the provision of money and people for the faith missions), providence became an integral and distinctive part of the Evangelical tradition.

Preaching

Worship is an important aspect of every Christian tradition. For the Evangelical, worship is marked by the preaching of the Word, the singing of hymnody, which reflects the personal relationship of the believer with Christ, and expectant prayer. Other elements may be present including liturgical form and celebration of the sacraments. Worship for the Evangelical is both *objective* – the declaration of the gospel and of praise to God – and *subjective*, an expression of an experiential relationship with Jesus. In the modern Evangelical tradition these experiential aspects have taken on a variety of forms ranging from testimony to the exercise of the Charismatic gifts.

The preaching of the Word has historically been the central element. This has been challenged in the modern age from both within the tradition (increasing the emphasis on experience) and outside the tradition (increasing the emphasis on the sacraments). During the Revival it was the preaching of the Word of 'new birth' that led to the new birth. The great preachers, from Whitefield to Spurgeon, preached for conversion, preached to teach and preached because they believed that the living authoritative Word of God had unique capacity to change lives. They preached at length and expected both attention and response. After all, both preacher and hearer were under the authority of the Word.

At The Eclectic Society, John Clayton stressed that all preaching should give equal weight to doctrinal, experiential and practical preaching, addressing mind, heart and life respectively.[33] Foster stated that the main problem was that of not stating doctrine.[34] John Newton described doctrine as the trunk and Thomas Scott said that doctrine must be scripturally stated and not reliant on experience.[35] Style has, of course, varied over time and has been adjusted to the occasion. However, a clear commitment to the exposition of the Scriptures in the sermon has, and remains, a distinctive of the Evangelical tradition.

Mission

It would seem axiomatic to say that mission is an Evangelical distinctive. It depends on the understanding of mission. Evangelicals were not the first to establish missions to bring the gospel to others. Monastic missions, Catholic missions, Anglican missions and Puritan missions all feature prior to Evangelical mission. Yet the missionary enterprise has become inextricably linked to Evangelical witness. What is the basis for this and what is distinctive about the Evangelical contribution? Common to the missionary enterprise of all Christians is their understanding of God as a God of mission, in which they are called to share; the *missio Dei*. This has usually been accompanied by a recognition that all humanity needs to be brought within the reach of the gospel. Sometimes the missionary impulse has also been accompanied by particular denominational or cultural expressions of the gospel. Evangelicals have not been exempt from this characteristic. Similarly the missionary enterprise has sometimes been directed more at society and its improvement rather than individual conversion. What is distinctive about mission for the Evangelical?

First, mission is evangelistic. There is specific purpose to Evangelical missionary enterprise. It is aimed at conversion, the message of new birth, the adding of individuals into the Church of God. It is not concerned with the spread of a culture or of a church denomination, even if these issues have become confused at times in Evangelical history. Hence, the preaching of the Word has traditionally been central to such missionary enterprise.

Second, mission is urgent and imperative. It is an imperative because evangelism is undertaken by Evangelicals as a direct response in obedience to the demands of the gospel – Matthew 28.20, the Great Commission. The expectation of evangelism is urgent because without the gospel there is only death (spiritual and ultimately physical) and separation from God. Heaven and hell are real alternatives for the Evangelical and emphasize the urgency of bringing the message of new birth to bear upon those who have yet to hear it.

Third, mission is catholic and interdenominational. Evangelism is so important, of the very essence of the gospel, that the particular tenets of church government must never be allowed to stand in the way. Evangelism is essentially catholic. It is the gospel that is being transmitted. To do so effectively and with the priority that is accorded to evangelism within Evangelicalism requires the cooperation of Evangelicals across the boundaries of denomination and culture. This is a practical expression of Evangelical catholicity. One of the earliest examples was the Bible Society founded in 1804 in which Evangelicals from across the denominational divide united around the common task of the distribution of the Scriptures. Evangelicals will join together in evangelistic campaigns, associations and societies. Inter-denominational missionary societies are invariably Evangelical.

Fourth, mission is faith driven. Over the course of history, Evangelicals have adopted a variety of methods in respect of mission, not without criticism from within the movement. For example in the early days of the CMS there was much criticism (not least under the influence of premillennialism) of its apparent reliance on human means and its unsustainable optimism. As part of the reaction to this, there emerged the development of faith missions (e.g. the China Inland Mission, later the Overseas Missionary Fellowship), which gave explicit emphasis to dependency upon God in the operations of the mission, not least in respect of the provision of both finance and personnel.

Mission, of course, has become a word embraced by all. The danger of this is that the definition is stretched in order to accommodate every possible understanding. For the Evangelical the distinctive features of mission are its evangelistic nature, its imperative and urgency, its catholicity and its faith basis.

Excursus on the atonement

The atonement – the meaning of the death of Jesus on the cross – is central to Evangelical identity. In both historical and contemporary context that which has become known as the penal substitutionary theory of the atonement is the defining characteristic of the cross for the Evangelical. Yet this understanding has been challenged not only from without, but also from within the Evangelical movement. It is important to understand a number of things:

- The nature of the critique
- Ensuring a proper appreciation of the Evangelical position
- Understanding the source of both revisionist and traditionalist approaches to the atonement

The nature of the critique
The cross divides. The cross defines. Almost all Evangelicals, as indeed most Christians, would agree on the centrality of the cross; where they would disagree is over the means of how the

cross impacts on the faith and the life of the individual believer. Throughout history differing understandings have been advanced. These have ranged from the cross as example, the cross as representative, the cross as the victory of Christ and the cross as substitute. Evangelical theology has never denied the first three of these,[36] but has always maintained that none of them makes sense unless interpreted through the primacy of the cross as substitute. Interestingly, critiques of Evangelicalism usually deny the substitutionary motif.

In 2003 the objections to the classic exposition of the cross were expounded again by Steve Chalke, a prominent Baptist minister, and Alan Mann.[37] This was subsequently built upon by both authors in articles, interviews and books. These objections also reflected the more radical elements of the Evangelical movement (from the nineteenth century through the 'liberal evangelicalism' of the 1920s, parts of the modern Charismatic movement and some prominent academics). The outline of the critique (to which Chalke and Mann's book contributed) is that the substitutionary atonement:

- Changes God from a loving Father into an angry, vengeful tyrant
- Expounds a view of 'redemptive violence'
- Contradicts the character of God ('God is love')
- Separates the persons of the Trinity from the community of the Trinity
- Turns Jesus into an enemy
- Contradicts the teaching of Jesus ('love your enemies')
- Emphasizes universal sin rather than human goodness
- Impacts on Christian mission in a negative fashion
- Encourages an image of Evangelicals as harsh and lacking grace
- Is ultimately unjust, since it is unjust to knowingly punish one person for another's crimes

The concern is to reclaim what is seen as an Evangelical over-emphasis on the details of the work of Christ upon the cross into a wider understanding of God's character and mission.

The dangers are that God's character and emotions become compartmentalized (so love and anger are separated) and that Evangelicalism becomes detached from its biblical roots.

Appreciating and understanding the substitutionary atonement

The challenge to the substitutionary atonement may, in fact, be of a 'straw man' rather than what Evangelicals actually believe and profess. However, it may also be that Evangelicals, either through laziness or lack of precision, have contributed to this misrepresentation. The following elements are critical in understanding the classic exposition of the atonement:

- Sin is universal and must be dealt with by God for forgiveness to be effective
- Substitution is to be understood within the Trinity, not outside it ('the self-substitution of God')
- God's character also involves *anger* (at sin) and *justice* (sin requires response) as well as *love*
- Sacrifice and propitiation (turning aside God's anger) are fundamental atonement metaphors in the Bible
- The cross shorn of penalty and substitute is not a cross of love and forgiveness
- It is the very transfer of our sin and penalty to Christ on the cross that effects both our forgiveness and our response
- The cross involving penalty and substitute is the understanding most consistent with both Old Testament and New Testament expositions of the meaning of the death of Jesus

The danger has been the separation of the persons of the Trinity and perhaps some emphasis on the definition of a theory ('penal substitution') that has also detached the meaning from its biblical roots. This understanding of the cross remains central to Evangelical self-definition; the terms of the definition, however, must be understood and expounded only insofar as is permitted from the pages of Scripture. The best modern treatments have been those of John Stott and also the classic work of Leon Morris.[38]

Sources of the alternative approaches

Why have these differences arisen and what is their source? Intellectually the response can be seen as the impact upon Evangelicalism of:

- The Enlightenment
- Romanticism
- Elements of Charismatic renewal
- Loss of identity

Bebbington emphasized that the movement was deeply effected by the successive waves of the prevailing intellectual currents of thought in the eighteenth and nineteenth centuries. The impact of Enlightenment rationalism was to expose Evangelical thought to the same influences as those which led to the development of a more rationalist, liberal Protestantism. In time this gave birth to a more liberal version of the Evangelical tradition, prominent in the first part of the twentieth century. Substitutionary atonement was one of the first victims. However, subsequent to Enlightenment rationality was the influence of Romanticism, with its emphasis on beauty, intimacy, the senses, visions of perfection, past and future. With a renewed concern for devotion and discipleship, encounter with and surrender to God, it was easy for the specifics of the cross (which were decidedly unromantic) to fade. The influence of Romanticism has been carried over into Charismatic renewal. As will be seen subsequently, Evangelicalism is a spectrum and those most influenced by the holiness traditions find expression in the modern Charismatic movement. Some elements of this movement have been influenced less by the Puritan emphasis on sin and atonement. It is particularly noticeable that the early generations of leaders of the Charismatic renewal remained firmly committed to the biblical foundations of Word and cross; it is less clear that will be the case with subsequent generations. In a sense all of this is a reflection of the widening nature of the Evangelical movement and its struggle with and even loss of identity.

Understanding the spiritual heritage

Perhaps something of the picture of Evangelicalism is emerging, based around the four focal points we have developed. In other words, a picture centred upon Scripture and its authority, the cross and its doctrinal heart, Jesus Christ, and our personal encounter with him and the missionary imperative with its transforming power. However, we know that the Evangelical tradition has a wide range of expressions today. If we can understand more about that heritage and what goes spiritually into making an Evangelical, we can appreciate both the diversity and the unity of the tradition.

Sources of influence and ways of expression

We noted earlier that the traditional background to understanding the Evangelical Revival and its emergence were the three strands of Puritan theology, High Church orthodoxy and reaction against rationalism. More recent formulations have referred to the influence of Puritanism, Pietism and Pentecostalism. All of these approaches have both attractions and complexities. The main difficulty lies in seeing these various lines of influence as operating in separate spheres. In fact the distinctive beauty of Evangelicalism lies in their interaction. In understanding how these aspects of the spiritual tradition relate to each other, we will increase both our appreciation of the heritage itself and our ability to understand Evangelicalism today. Perhaps the best way of describing the spiritual sources of Evangelicalism are:

- The Reformation foundations
- The Pietist heritage
- The Holiness tradition

The Reformation foundations

We have already pointed out the roots of Evangelicalism in the Reformation principles of the authority of Scripture and justification by faith. The Reformation was of critical importance to the later development of Evangelicalism. It was in the Reformation, its course and aftermath, that the foundational principles of the later

Evangelical tradition were established. Evangelicalism gives significant weight to the key doctrinal emphases of the Reformation. As the Reformation developed, many of these doctrinal emphases were continued by the later Puritan tradition. There were some distinctive elements and some important landmarks along the way. The Puritan sought the purity of the gospel and the purity of the teaching of Scripture. The aim was to apply the explicit demands of Scripture to the Church and to the worship of the Church in the sense that only what was explicitly sanctioned in Scripture could be countenanced.

The doctrines which characterized the Reformed and Puritan traditions were the authority of Scripture, the total depravity of humanity, God's grace and justification by faith through the atoning sacrifice of Christ upon the cross. To these were added a view of Church and sacraments that emphasized faithful reception rather than presence and a ministry of teaching and preaching. Other doctrinal aspects also featured including a developed covenant theology, the double decree of predestination and anti-Catholicism. The spiritual marks were characterized by systematic Bible reading, expository preaching, doctrinal treatises, godly order and discipline and an understanding of holiness in the Christian life that gave weight and significance to conflict with the world and with sin in our daily lives.

The Pietist heritage

The Reformation itself had different strands and emphases. One of these was what has become known as the Radical Reformation. Various groups sought out an active holiness of life that gave centrality to believers' baptism, the spiritualization and internalization of the Word, and the development of separate communities of the true Church, apart from the world of sin and evil. These disparate groups, mainly on the continent of Europe, developed in a number of directions. They set the scene for the later development of Pietist groups in the sixteenth and seventeenth centuries. The early leaders were Philipp Spener (1635–1705) and August Francke (1663–1727). This was a religion of the heart, a stirring based upon the experience of a personal encounter with Jesus Christ, leading to action, not least in the social sphere through, for example, the founding of orphanages. Emphasis was given to the fellowship of the people of God, the community of the saved. Those called by Christ were to be dependent upon him in their daily lives.

Among those influenced by this renewed pietistic faith were Count Nikolas von Zinzendorf (1700–1760) and the Moravian Church. Von Zinzendorf reacted against the dry Protestant orthodoxy of the seventeenth century. He founded the pietistic Herrnhut community in 1722 on his estate. It was a Moravian missionary, ordained by von Zinzendorf, Peter Böhler, who travelled to England and encountered the Wesleys. John Wesley met Böhler on several occasions, including upon Wesley's own return from Georgia in January 1738. Wesley recorded in his diary Böhler's emphasis on the two inseparable fruits of true faith in Christ, namely dominion over sin and peace from a sense of forgiveness.[39] The early history of Evangelicalism captures the emphasis well:

> Both [Böhler and Wesley] accepted St Paul's teaching that the Christian is saved by faith, but faith to Wesley was a very complicated and complex thing, a process mainly intellectual . . . To Böhler it was simple reliance on the finished work of Christ.[40]

Wesley's conversion narrative followed in May 1738 clearly reflecting the arrival of pietistic encounter into Reformed theology.

The Holiness tradition

Investigations of the sources of Evangelical spirituality give some weight to the Pentecostal strand. However, in many ways this is an anachronism, a reading back of a more modern expression of Evangelicalism into the heritage of the tradition. Many similar elements were present in the early pietistic emphases of encounter and dependence. However, in the nineteenth century, through what has become known as the Holiness Movement, these ideas were further development into the themes of intimacy and surrender. The Holiness Movement grew out of a distinctive approach to sanctification. Its origins lay in the Wesleyan understanding of the possibility of entire sanctification, a total death to sin, this side of heaven. The idea was further developed by Phoebe Palmer who, as Bebbington notes, urged believers to lay all on the altar.[41] We see here the move from dependence to surrender. All that was needed was faith. The teaching spread beyond its original Methodist origins. Full salvation and sanctification were possible through submission in faith to the Holy Spirit. In both America and England the movement spread through revivalist camp meetings. The Holiness Movement tended also to a separatist mentality – separation from the corruption of the Church. Increasing emphasis was given to full salvation, intimacy and surrender before God and baptism in the Holy Spirit.

In England one particular expression of the Holiness Movement was through the founding and development of the Keswick Convention. Keswick, like the Holiness Movement more widely, was closely related to the prevailing romanticism of the mid-Victorian era. William Pennefather, through the Mildmay Conference, brought together those concerned for evangelism, revival and personal consecration. Bebbington points out the note of surrender to the Lord, quoting from one adherent of the higher life, Robert Pearsall Smith, who maintained that holiness consisted 'simply in ceasing from all efforts of our own, and trusting Jesus'.[42] In 1874 the first Keswick Convention was held with a week of meetings emphasizing practical holiness.

This assessment of the sources of the Evangelical spiritual heritage, with all its complexity, can be expressed diagrammatically in a way that helps explain and understand the Evangelical tradition in both its historic and modern expression (see page 80).

The starting point is the Word of God. This, as we have seen, lies at the very heart of Evangelicalism, its centrality, authority and clarity. From the Bible is drawn the cross of Christ, the atoning sacrifice of Jesus. Two aspects of the antecedents of Evangelicalism now come into play. On the one hand, there is the body of Reformed Protestant doctrine, forming an essential feature of the Evangelical tradition as mediated through the Puritan tradition. On the other hand, there is the Pietist emphasis on personal encounter with Jesus. The key point for understanding the nature of Evangelicalism is the recognition that both these elements derive from the Bible and the cross and form crucial aspects in Evangelicalism. In understanding the modern expressions of the movement, the greater the emphasis placed upon Protestant doctrine the closer the adherent will be to the Reformed end of Evangelicalism. By way of contrast, the more weight that is given

Evangelical Spiritual Heritage

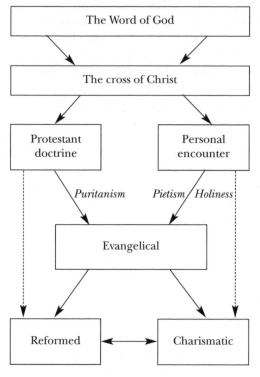

to the personal encounter with, and dependence upon, Christ, the closer will be the person to the Charismatic expression of the Evangelical tradition. This is affected by the varying understanding of experience, assurance and response to the quest for holiness. Hence most Evangelicals are somewhere on a spectrum reflecting the relative influence of the antecedent traditions between the Reformed and the Charismatic.

A fuller appreciation is gained by recognizing that there are strands of influence of the prior traditions that are not mediated through Evangelicalism. Thus the body of Protestant doctrine can be expressed without the influence of the personal experiential encounter particular to Evangelicalism in either a nationalistic Protestantism, a state Protestantism or an exclusivist Calvinism as in the closed Brethren. Similarly the emphasis on personal encounter, intimacy and, not just dependence upon Christ but the holiness concern for surrender, can pass down into part of the modern Charismatic movement without the doctrinal influences of the Reformed tradition. This would be expressed in a Charismatic mysticism, an embracing of sacramentalism and symbolism. This might lead, for example, to a spiritual affinity and unity with Roman Catholicism or spill over into New Age spirituality, or perhaps an unthinking adoption of Celtic spiritual influences.

The Evangelical way of holiness

The various spiritual influences which have gone to make up Evangelicalism have somewhat different understandings of aspects of holiness. We see this expressed in the varying impact of experience on the Christian life, with differing approaches to Christian assurance. This varying influence can be illustrated by Puritan classics such as John Bunyan's *Pilgrim's Progess*, and by the development of faith missions, drawing upon the more pietistic and pentecostal traditions of Evangelicalism. The strength of the Puritan vision of the Christian life, as set out in Bunyan's influential description of the pilgrim, Christian, is its recognition that this world cannot be avoided but must be travelled through, as a pilgrim. There is a certainty of destination, but constant temptation and need for faithfulness, not least to the Word of God itself. Thus the Puritan vision has tended to view our whole life's journey as spiritual, so that our work in the world has deep spiritual significance, not just our religious work. This reflects the Reformation emphasis (for example, Luther's idea of calling, and the value he attached to household work over and against an exalted view of the monastic life). It is also part of the background to the development of the Protestant work ethic. The problem was that this also led to a life of angst about sin and the need for constant diligence. Assurance of salvation was always in danger of being clouded by the conflicts of daily life. This understanding is a *progressive* view of sanctification. In other words, the living out of the Christian life as a means to and expression of holiness is a gradual process, a daily conflict with sin, and perfection will not be reached in this life. Those more influenced by the Pietist and Holiness traditions adopt approaches to sanctification and the Christian life that represent a more *instantaneous* and *interventionist* methodology. In various ways this is reflected in moderate form in Wesleyan perfectionism (that Christian perfection is achievable in this life), in the separation of the holy from the world (even in Keswick) and through the continued presence and empowerment of the Holy Spirit – baptism in the Spirit.

Thus the Christian life in the Pietist tradition is often characterized by submission to God and in the Holiness tradition by surrender to God, reflected in the handing over of all aspects of daily life to the Lord. This leads to much greater weight being placed upon divine means rather than human means, upon his daily acts of intervention in special acts of providence and of continued empowerment of the believer by the surrender of their life to the Lord. In the light of an interventionist Christ there was nothing humans could do – except of course submit and surrender. In response to this trend a new emphasis was given to interdenominational faith missions, the dominant characteristic of which was dependence neither upon human means nor human institutions (the Church) but only upon the Lord, for money, for revival – in response to prayer and indeed for daily provision. This view had enormous impact upon Evangelicalism, reflected in both individuals such as George Müller of Bristol, and Hudson Taylor and missions such as the China Inland Mission.

Thus can be seen the various approaches to holiness from those elements that go to make up Evangelicalism. It is important to appreciate both the various antecedents and the differing emphasis placed upon them at different times. It is also important to understand that Evangelicalism and its diversity derives from the interaction of these varying aspects and the relative significance placed upon them. That is its unique contribution to the Christian tradition and that helps in our understanding of the nature and variety of expression of the Evangelical tradition today.

Evangelicals and the Church: the quest for holiness

Evangelicals have a passion for holiness which extends beyond the individual into the Church, its organization and worship. This is due, at least in part, to the priority afforded in the Evangelical understanding of the Church to the invisible Church (the community of the elect) over the visible Church (the present gathering of the local church). This concern is greatest in those Evangelicals who owe most to the Puritan heritage. During the Elizabethan era the Puritan party constantly pressed for the organization and worship of the Church to reflect only that which was expressly permitted in Scripture. The Elizabethan settlement had been based upon a Reformed Protestant doctrinal settlement, but with a degree of flexibility over matters of practice when Scripture was silent. Puritans down the ages have always been very sure of what the Scripture taught, though when put into practice the clarity has somewhat diminished.

The shift of emphasis in Evangelical theology in the 1820s gave renewed weight to the quest for holiness. As we shall see, the increased criticism of the prevailing theology of Evangelicalism (concerned with human means, human power and influence, loss of passion for God's righteousness) and the significance of the growth of an interventionist premillennialism (in its various forms) all contributed to this spiritual longing for purity.

CMS, founded in 1799, originally as 'The Society for Missions to Africa and the East', was the brainchild and the flagship of the early Evangelicals in the Church of England. It reflected both the theological emphases of early Evangelicalism and some of the intellectual and cultural currents at the time. Over the first 20 years of its existence it placed a degree of weight upon the human responsibility for the spread of the gospel, an optimistic outlook for its success and a theological postmillennialism that saw the Church moving gradually towards the blessed future which the Lord had in store. From around 1820 onwards there was something of a theological shift within Evangelicalism. Optimism gave way to pessimism (about both the world and the Church), human means to divine means and the Lord's overall general providence to an interventionist special providence. Indeed theologically a form of interventionist premillennialism became the dominant theme. The details are complex and the description and analysis of the range of views on the millennium at the time rarely understood.[43] In essence what was at stake was the understanding of the 1,000-year reign of Christ in Revelation 20.

We need to set out something of the range of views:

- Historicist premillennialism; in moderate and extreme form
- Futurist (dispensationalist) premillennialism
- Gradualist postmillennialism
- Amillennialism

Historicist premillennialists asserted the return of Christ prior to the millennium (hence, 'premillennial') which would inaugurate the 1,000 years (almost always interpreted literally) of peace and blessedness. The Book of Revelation was the guide, and if we were somewhere in the region of Chapter 20 (where the millennium appears) then it must be possible to map the rest of the book on to the course of human history (hence 'historicist'). In its more extreme form this involved a detailed plotting of events, including the association of the complex symbolism of Revelation with human personalities and events, and the calculation of a date for the return of Christ. The more moderate form of this approach embraced the principle but not the detail. There was most certainly a concern for 'the signs of the times', pointers to the pessimistic decline of humanity and the prevalence of sin as indicators of the end times. There was no concern here with the details of date setting.

Futurist or dispensational premillennialists also advocated a premillennial Second Advent. However, this view saw human history as divided up into distinct eras or dispensations; the events of Revelation largely belonged to the future, the final dispensation of the millennium to be introduced by the 'rapture'. Hence the millennium, though preceded by the second advent, lay at some undescribed future point.

Gradualist postmillennialism saw gradual improvement brought about in society (so society would be always improving as would personal morality) and a general optimism concerning future prospects. This optimism and improvement was brought about due to the progress and impact of the gospel. As humanity and its setting improved, so gradually we would enter the blessedness and peace of the millennium, at the end of which (and it might be a literal 1,000 years or a figurative long period of time), Christ would return.

For completeness, amillennialism should be mentioned, which, although it has many moderate modern Evangelical adherents, had few advocates in the formative period of the nineteenth century, and certainly not with the modern terminology. This view saw the whole period of time between the first coming and the second coming (at an indeterminate time in the future) as representing the millennium. Hence the events of human history could not be fitted to the symbolism of Revelation, the gospel was to be preached, pessimism and optimism would both be present and Christ would return.

All of this was also exemplified by the crises in the Bible Society in 1825–27 over the Apocrypha and in 1830–31 over doctrinal tests. Evangelicals fell out over the Bible and prayer. The details can be read elsewhere.[44] In outline the first clash was over the inclusion of the Apocrypha in editions of the Bible for circulation in Roman Catholic countries where this was the only way to gain circulation for the Scriptures. The issue was a narrow one, but then the quest for purity is often exceedingly narrow. Was the pure, undiluted Word of God to take priority over the demands of Christian mission in one or two specific instances of difficulty? The answer in the new, purer atmosphere of the 1820s was in the affirmative, though the Evangelical doyen Charles Simeon was amongst the dissenters. The second conflict concerned, first of all, the desirability of opening meetings in prayer and then more explicitly moves to ensure membership of the society was reserved for Trinitarian Christians. The movers of these resolutions, J. E. Gordon, founder in 1827 of the British (later Protestant) Reformation Society, and the prominent Evangelical, Baptist Noel, were, on this occasion defeated. This led to the foundation of the Trinitarian Bible Society in 1831 by a rather strange combination of theological premillennialists and high-Tory national Protestants. What was at stake in this debate? First, the Evangelical concern for truth. Second, a desire for the Church militant on earth to reflect that truth in its life and practice. Third, an understanding of the character of God as holy and that such holiness should be reflected in both personal and corporate life.

What is less clear is exactly how pure purity needs to be, where the boundaries are to be set. The outcome of such debates is that rarely are the solutions proposed pure enough for all concerned. This then leads to division and separation, the antithesis of the catholicity that belongs to the essence of Evangelicalism. It is also the case that even the divisions that result from such conflicts are rarely pure. When the Trinitarian Bible Society was founded, many Evangelicals remained with the Bible Society, others ran dual membership and some later returned to the parent body. Interestingly, as time went on, the Bible Society began to adopt many of the practices that had been demanded by the proponents of doctrinal tests. The same phenomenon is observable in the

twentieth century with the split in the CMS which gave birth to
BCMS. Indeed, one of the features of the Puritan part of the
Church throughout the history of its relationship with the wider
Church of England is that, on every occasion when there was
division, there were those who stayed and laboured as well as those
who departed.

So Evangelicalism has always been passionate for the truth and
has not seen the visible Church as being somehow excluded from
that passion. The history shows that tension between truth and
unity has affected the Evangelical movement itself as well as its
relationships with others. The way in which such tensions are
responded to and handled reflects the relative influence of the
antecedent traditions as well as contemporary awareness of
Evangelical identity and heritage.

Evangelicalism today

How is all of this reflected in modern, contemporary Evangelicalism? The various influences, historic antecedents and current
emphases are all represented, and perhaps can now be better
understood. In the common core is a biblical doctrinal emphasis
and a commitment to church growth and evangelism. This sits
within a contemporary expression of worship, ranging from the
more objective (centred on God's character and work) to the
more subjective (based upon our intimacy, dependence and
personal response to God). In the latter case, sung worship in
intimate fashion would feature as a significant aspect of worship.
Preaching would be central but the emphasis of preaching would
range from expository and doctrinal (at the Reformed end of the
spectrum) to more experiential (at the charismatic), although, of
course, these things are not mutually exclusive. In the wider life of
the Church, the Reformed would be characterized by teaching,
discipleship, mission and prayer with an objective understanding
of God, his character, his holiness and his righteousness. The
Charismatic expression of church life would see weight given to a
more subjective understanding of God, an expectancy of intervention in the life of the believer (healing prayer, spiritual gifts)
and an intimacy with the Lord. There is much overlap and, as has
been demonstrated, there is a spectrum of Evangelical belief and
practice.

A commitment to church growth and the planting of new congregations is another expression of the contemporary Evangelical movement. We see this within both Reformed and charismatic traditions. The nature of church planting ranges from establishing new congregations within existing churches to new churches in pioneering situations (see case study in Chapter 3). In these respects the Evangelical movement is often seen as being placed at the cutting edge of church growth and development. That is not to say that other Christian traditions do not plant or grow, but rather that this is a particular characteristic of contemporary Evangelicalism. The range of modern Evangelical spirituality can also be seen in the approaches to holiness and Christian living. Both the Reformed and the charismatic dimensions of Evangelicalism emphasize holiness of life. For the more Reformed this will be seen in an emphasis upon repentance from sin, a mind conformed to God's will, fear of God, obedience, a life of struggling against sin, demonstrating the fruits of the Spirit and faithfulness. It is not that these emphases are absent from the more charismatic expressions of the Christian life, though due to a more interventionist view of God greater weight is given to intimacy with Christ, resting in him and an empowering by him. This would be illustrated not only in spiritual gifts but also in spiritual disciplines. More significance would be attached to fasting, simplicity of life, submission, special guidance and celebration. There may also be interest in more Catholic spiritual practices that would be rejected by the more Reformed. Variations may include liturgical patterns of worship, variety of frequency of Communion and how the Christian Church relates to the wider community.

Hence, in understanding Evangelicalism today in its contemporary form, it is important to recognize both the central core and the variety that exists around that essential heart of the tradition. Tensions arise over the nature of God, his revelation, the contemporary expression of God's intervention, varying emphasis on sin and the nature of the Christian life and the implications for the Church. All of this is more easily understood and properly weighed in the light of the history of the Evangelical tradition.

Question and Answer – Evangelicalism

What are the key features of Evangelicalism?
Evangelicalism can be described in three main ways. First, a
generalist approach, which seeks to embrace the breadth of
those who claim the name Evangelical. Second, a propositional approach – a detailed list of beliefs and practices.
Third, sociological method which describes centres, groups
or themes around which Evangelicals gather. A more
fruitful approach is to look at four spiritual centres for
the Evangelical. These are authority (the Bible), doctrine
(the substitutionary atonement), spirituality (new birth,
personal relationship) and transformation (evangelism
and changing society). The distinctives of Evangelicalism
could be summarized as Bible, Cross, Christ and Mission,
but it is important to note that it is the particulars of belief
that characterize the Evangelical, not the generalities.

Do Evangelicals believe in the Bible literally?
Yes . . . and no! Evangelicals are united that the Bible is the
revealed Word of God. The Bible is the supreme and final
authority in all matters of faith and life. It is not equal with
other approaches (tradition or reason or experience); it is
both complete and sufficient. Traditionally, Evangelicals have
given great weight to the direct inspiration of the very words
of Scripture. This has become known (but was not so originally) as plenary inspiration. Words such as infallible and
inerrant have also been used to describe the perfection and
authority of the Bible. However, this assertion does not mean
a wooden literalism that fails to take account of the various
genres of the biblical material (poetry is not to be read the
same way as narrative). The Evangelical is always conscious
that we do not possess the originals of the Scriptures, only
copies. Hence there is a task of interpretation. Although this
must be understood with a provisionality, it must also be
approached with humility before the gracious and holy Lord
who has revealed his Word to us, to which we must submit. We
need also to remember that the revelation of the Word has a

transparency and perspicuity; in other words, there is one clear message, capable of discernment to the ordinary reader of the text. The Evangelical approach to interpretation starts with the plain meaning of the written Word.

How do you explain the varieties of Evangelicalism?
Evangelicalism is a spectrum. We have described the common core deriving from the Bible as the Word of God. However, the differing weight attached to doctrine or to personal encounter with Christ, affected by the relative significance of the Puritan, Pietist or Holiness approach to the Christian life, will lead to a different place on the spectrum. It is the varying emphasis placed on these factors that leads to differing expressions of the Evangelical tradition. In extreme instances the impact of the Puritan doctrinal heritage or the Pietist/ Holiness traditions can bypass the Evangelical tradition all together.

How is Evangelical spirituality expressed?
In a wide variety of ways reflecting the various background streams. For the more Reformed the emphasis will be on the objective worship of God and the objective teaching of God, expressing his character and holiness. The more Charismatic will give weight to the intimate encounter with God and give emphasis to personal encounter in prayer, healing and spiritual disciplines.

Why can't Evangelicals get on with others?
Well, they can . . . and, there again, they can't! There are both positive and negative aspects to this question. On one level Evangelical ecclesiology (that is, the understanding of the Church) permits a much greater level of cooperation than is either sometimes admitted, or achieved by those with a more particular denominational outlook. Evangelicalism encourages a unity that crosses both cultures and denominations. This is seen at every level of church life, from local church, to conferences and alliances (for example, The Evangelical Alliance), to mission societies and to global interaction.

However, as we have seen, Evangelicalism is also marked by *doctrinal* commitment and also a quest for *purity* in the life of the Church. The unity that characterizes Evangelicalism is 'unity in the truth'. What is more, the importance of the confessional nature of the Christian faith to the Evangelical, alongside the injunctions of Scripture against false teaching, leads Evangelicals to reject association with the doctrinally heterodox. This is heightened when issues under debate relate to the heart of Evangelical Christian identity: the Bible, the cross, Jesus Christ, the task of mission. When the whole of that weight is applied to the quest for purity, doctrinal exactitude may predominate over Evangelical catholicity and lead to increased internal disagreement.

Notes

1   The Earl of Shaftesbury, quoted in E. Hodder (1892), *The Life and Work of the Seventh Earl of Shaftesbury K.G.*, London, Cassells, p. 738.

2   P. Brierley (2000), *The Tide is Running Out*, London, Christian Research (and associated publications).

3   M. A. Noll (2004), *The Rise of Evangelicalism*, Leicester, Apollos is the most recent comprehensive treatment.

4   J. D. Walsh (1966), 'Origins of the Evangelical Revival', in G. V. Bennett and J. D. Walsh, *Essays in Modern English Church History*, New York, Oxford University Press.

5   J. C. D. Clark (2000), *English Society 1688–1832*, 2nd edition, Cambridge, Cambridge University Press.

6   D. W. Bebbington (1989), *Evangelicalism in Modern Britain*, London, Unwin Hyman, p. 6.

7   Noll, op. cit., p. 12.

8   The Revd W. R. Nicholson (1875), *Reasons Why I Became A Reformed Episcopalian*, Philadelphia.

9   Note the resignation of The Revd Roland Allen from the living of Chalfont St Peter, quoted in C. O. Buchanan (1993), *Infant Baptism and the Gospel*, London, Darton Longman & Todd.

10   Bebbington, op. cit., pp. 2–17.

11   Ibid., p. 3.

12   Ibid., p. 14.

13   J. I. Packer (1978), *The Evangelical Anglican Identity Problem*, Oxford, Latimer Studies 1, Latimer House, pp. 20–3, restated by A. E. McGrath (1994), *Evangelicalism and the Future of Christianity*, London, Hodder and Stoughton, p. 51.

14 Bebbington, op.cit., p. 218.
15 D. F. Wells (1994), 'On Being Evangelical' in M. A. Noll, D. W. Bebbington and G. A. Rawlyk, *Evangelicalism*, New York, Oxford University Press, pp. 389–410.
16 This work builds upon R. D. Turnbull (1999), 'Evangelicalism: the state of scholarship and the question of identity', *Anvil* vol. 16, no. 2.
17 J. H. Pratt (ed.), (1865), *The Thought of the Evangelical Leaders: notes of the discussions of The Eclectic Society, London during the years 1798–1814*, reprinted, 1978, Edinburgh, Banner of Truth.
18 Pratt, op.cit., p. 153.
19 Ibid., p. 154.
20 Ibid., p. 153.
21 Ibid., p. 154.
22 Ibid., p. 133.
23 P. Toon (1979), *Evangelical Theology 1833–1856*, London, Marshall, Morgan and Scott.
24 Ibid., p. 128.
25 D. Peterson (2006), 'The Bible in a Postmodern Age,' in C. Green (ed.), *Guarding the Gospel*, Grand Rapids, Zondervan, p. 65.
26 D. L. Edwards and J. R. W. Stott (1988), *Essentials*, London, Hodder and Stoughton, p. 101.
27 J. Calvin, *Institutes of the Christian Religion*, Book II, 16.6, J. T. McNeill (ed.), Library of Christian Classics, Philadelphia, The Westminster Press.
28 Pratt, op.cit., p. 275.
29 Ibid., p. 167.
30 Ibid., p. 140.
31 Ibid., p. 468.
32 R. D. Turnbull (1997), *The place of the seventh Earl of Shaftesbury within the Evangelical tradition, with particular reference to his understanding of the relationship of evangelistic mission to social reform*, Durham, University of Durham Ph.D. thesis, p. 38.
33 Pratt, op.cit., p. 77.
34 Ibid.
35 Ibid.
36 D. Hilborn (2005), Introductory Address, Evangelical Alliance Symposium, 6–8 July 2005 draws attention to Recapitulation Theory (reversal of Adam's sin), Dramatic Theory (victory of Christ over evil) and Commercial Theory (Christ's honour redeeming human dishonour). All of these have featured in Evangelical thought.
37 S. Chalke and A. Mann (2003), *The Lost Message of Jesus*, Grand Rapids, Zondervan.
38 J. R. W. Stott (1986), *The Cross of Christ*, Leicester, IVP; L. Morris (1955), *The Apostolic Preaching of the Cross*, London, Tyndale Press.
39 J. Wesley, *Journal*, 24 May 1738.
40 G. R. Balleine (1909), *A History of the Evangelical Party in the Church of England*, London, Longmans, p. 23.
41 D. W. Bebbington (2005), *The Dominance of Evangelicalism*, Leicester, IVP, p. 190.
42 Ibid., p. 194.

43   R. D. Turnbull (1997), *The place of the seventh Earl of Shaftesbury within the Evangelical tradition, with particular reference to his understanding of the relationship of evangelistic mission to social reform,* Durham, University of Durham Ph.D. thesis, pp. 150–64, 203–30.

44   Ibid., pp. 157–64.

3

Anglican Evangelicalism

The quest for identity

This chapter is concerned with the essential features which have shaped and continue to form the identity of Anglican Evangelicalism. It is neither a detailed analysis of what Anglican Evangelicals might think about particular topics nor an attempt to synthesize all things Evangelical with all things Anglican. Our purpose is to pursue the matter of identity. What are the characteristics which bring Evangelical and Anglican together in one person? What points of engagement are there, and differences, between the wider Anglican and Evangelical movements?

The formation of identity for Anglican Evangelicals: moderate Calvinism

Anglican Evangelicals have an identity that is distinctive, faithful and honouring to the traditions from which it draws. That relationship is positive, creative and yet also not without both theological and practical tensions. The debate over terminology (Anglican Evangelical or Evangelical Anglican) was noted in the Introduction. The concern here is with relationship, engagement and difference, in respect of these two dynamic Christian traditions, and the distinctiveness of the Anglican Evangelical. There are a number of factors which contribute to the formation of Anglican Evangelical identity. The theological root of Anglican Evangelicalism can be summarized as 'moderate Calvinism'. This can be seen in the appeal to the Protestantism of the Thirty-Nine Articles, in the theological discussions of The Eclectic Society and expressed today in modern Anglican Evangelical scholarship. It brings together the continued Reformed or Puritan traditions alongside the insights of the Revival with a renewed spiritual heart, which chimes with the historic foundations of the Anglican tradition. The centrality of the cross, with the death of Christ understood as both substitutionary and as penal, has been a key defining feature of Evangelicalism. Anglican Evangelicals, in the aftermath of the disputes in the eighteenth century on the scope of the atonement, formed the position of the sufficiency of the atonement for all, but that the acceptance of the offer was not available to all. The offer of redemption was universal (*general redemption*). The covenant of grace was only available to those elect who were to be saved (*particular redemption*).

John Venn, the Vicar of Clapham, summarized the moderate Calvinism of Anglican Evangelicalism at The Eclectic Society:

> If to believe the truth of the gospel is enough, then all may be saved. If it be to believe savingly, then the range is more limited.[1]

This is the distinctively Anglican Evangelical handling of predestination. One nineteenth-century Evangelical leader, Daniel Wilson, described this as 'practical Calvinism'.[2] This meant the retention of the Calvinist stress on sin and depravity, and hence on the work of Christ upon the cross, but rather than a strict application of the benefits of the atonement only to the elect, stress on the sufficiency of the cross for all. This emphasis has been of significant importance for holding together the priority of evangelism alongside a Reformed doctrinal emphasis within Anglican Evangelicalism.

The same moderate Calvinism can be seen in modern Anglican Evangelical theological writing. The penal substitutionary understanding of the atonement is affirmed, indeed asserted as the central or controlling model of the atonement, by, for example, both John Stott and Peter Jensen. However, this is done within the context of a Trinitarian understanding of God, the self-satisfaction and self-substitution of God, who is indeed the initiator of propitiation.

> I am not saying that substitution is *the* one and only meaning of the cross, for the cross speaks of victory over evil, the revelation of love and glory through suffering. But if you are talking of atonement, the means by which we sinners can be reconciled to

the God of holy love, why, then, yes, I don't think you or I can escape the truth of the divine substitution.[3]

Article 17 also reflects this 'moderate Calvinism', with its concern with predestination to eternal life.

The application of practical Calvinism in doctrine, evangelism, ecclesiology and pastoral ministry is a significant characteristic of Anglican Evangelicalism. It combines the force of Evangelical doctrine with the openness and engagement of the wider Anglican tradition. Hence it provides both a firm base for identity and a clear partner for dialogue. It brings challenge to the wider Anglican tradition (the need for firm theological moorings) and is challenged by it (how to engage openly with a wider community).

Claiming the Prayer Book

The Book of Common Prayer used (or not, as the case may be) in the contemporary Church is that of 1662. However, appreciation of the antecedent prayer books is essential to any understanding of Anglican Evangelicalism. This is sometimes hard for the contemporary Anglican Evangelical to understand. This is for two reasons. First, in Churches influenced most by the Charismatic aspects of the Evangelical spiritual tradition there has been a tendency to depart from the common liturgical pattern of Anglicanism in favour of more contemporary, imaginative, creative and local expressions of worship. In some cases this has led to more varied and creative liturgical practice and in others to a much looser liturgical framework. To a degree this has been sanctioned by liturgical reform and renewal within the Church of England. Second, in more Reformed churches, the widespread pattern of postwar twentieth-century Anglican practice of a weekly Communion as the normal pattern of worship (which itself represents a discontinuity from historic Reformed Anglican practice) has meant the loss of a common 'Morning Prayer' service. These Churches, too, have adopted a more contemporary framework, whether in the context of Communion or Morning Worship. The impact in both instances has been to dilute the corporate memory of Anglican Evangelicalism.

Many appeal to the Prayer Book. First, the more conservative Evangelicals of the Church of England claim the heritage – it features as the first objective of the conservative Evangelical Church Society. Second, elements of the Anglo-Catholic constituency ('Prayer Book Catholics'), emboldened by the history and influence of the Oxford Movement, also look to the Prayer Book. The third group to appeal to the Prayer Book are traditionalists (perhaps represented in the Prayer Book Society) where the aim is more the preservation of the traditional form and language of common worship, as much as the doctrine contained within it. How is it possible for such different constituencies and groups to appeal to the same Prayer Book? The answer is, in essence, that they don't. Rather, these differing ecclesiastical expressions of modern Anglicanism actually appeal to different antecedent prayer books prior to the Book of Common Prayer of 1662. To be more precise, the various traditions give differing weight to those aspects of the Book of Common Prayer which derive from the prior volumes.

The essence of the appeal to the Prayer Book of the Anglican Evangelical is that the point of reference is actually to the second Prayer Book of Edward VI, the 1552 Prayer Book. Here is found the Reformed Anglican liturgy of the Protestant paradise, albeit short-lived. Foundational to that identity, and of particular importance to dialogue with wider Anglicanism, is the recognition that it was the 1552 Prayer Book which formed the basis of both the Elizabethan settlement and the 1662 Prayer Book. Although the Reformed basis of the 1549 Prayer Book should not be overlooked, other traditions give more weight to that particular book. The loss, or at least the dilution, of the historic memory of Anglican Evangelicals has been one of the elements which has led to the obscuring of identity. A word of caution and balance is necessary in case it should be thought that this is a partisan assertion. The existence of other Anglican traditions is also explained by a similar appeal. More Catholic Anglicans call upon the 1549 Prayer Book and those elements of 1549 which were reflected in the later books. Actually many Anglo-Catholics in their appeal to the Prayer Book reflect the amendments of the 1928 Prayer Book, rejected by Parliament. Traditionalists invoke the language and expression of the 1662 book; those of more liberal tradition appeal to the ambiguity and complexity of the 1662 book. The appeals to the various prayer books help us both explain and understand the diversity of traditions which form Anglicanism.

In the United States the problem is clearer in one respect and more obscure in another. Within Anglicanism in the USA there has been significantly less departure from the tradition of common prayer than has been the case in the United Kingdom. Hence the corporate memory of the importance of the Prayer Book tradition remains intact in more significant ways. This has been reflected in the retention of Morning Prayer as the principal Sunday service in 'lower' church parishes. However, the Protestant influence in the Episcopal Church of the USA has unquestionably become veiled, especially since the liturgical revisions of 1979. The history was noted earlier in Chapter 2. The Protestant tradition declined from 1873 onwards; lower churchmanship was often only nominally Protestant and the defence of Christianity as a revealed faith became the preserve of Anglo-Catholicism.[4]

The place of anti-Catholicism

An anti-Catholic strand has long influenced Anglican Evangelicalism.[5] This is true both externally (towards Rome) and internally (Anglo-Catholicism). The influence of this aspect of Evangelicalism has varied in different time periods and is perhaps less noticed in popular Anglican Evangelical belief today. However, anti-Catholicism can still unite Evangelicals on the General Synod on doctrinal grounds.[6] This is perhaps most noticeable in those strands of Evangelicalism influenced by the Reformed and Puritan traditions. To what extent does anti-Catholicism form an essential or peripheral part of Anglican Evangelical identity?

The starting point is to recall the importance of the Reformation as a foundation stone of the Anglican Evangelical tradition, expressed in the Prayer Books and the Thirty-Nine Articles of Religion. Hence part of the development of the tradition involves the assertion of a Reformed Protestant doctrine in contradistinction to Roman doctrinal thought. This is reflected in a number of anti-Roman Articles concerning the Mass, the Lord's Supper, justification, papal authority and jurisdiction (for example, Articles 19, 22, 25, 28, 31, 37). However, as the Evangelical tradition emerged in the light of the Revival, anti-Romanism was not prominent. Doctrine, including the discussions at The Eclectic Society, were clearly Protestant but did not focus upon specifically anti-Catholic matters. The Eclectic Society did not, for example, discuss the

Lord's Supper. This position changed in three ways in the mid-nineteenth century.[7]

First, there were renewed doctrinal emphases within Evangelicalism which strengthened the Protestant doctrine underlying the tradition. This is primarily shown by the development of premillennialism as a dominant feature within Evangelicalism. This encouraged speculation over the identity of the anti-Christ, the beast of the Book of Revelation. Although there were a variety of candidates, including Napoleon, Evangelicals increasingly identified the anti-Christ with Rome and the papacy. Although this was not without precedent both at the time of the Reformation and afterwards, it came to a new prominence.

Second, with the rise of the Oxford Movement, there was a reaction against Catholic tendencies within the Church of England, especially in the areas of authority, justification, the Church and the Supper. We have already noted in Chapter 2 the details of the theological reaction of Evangelicals to the Tractarian Movement. Evangelical doctrinal positions did not change but in some respects were strengthened. Priority came to be given to matters of Church and sacraments where Tractarians seemed to be going well beyond the accepted positions of the Protestant Reformation. Subsequently this position hardened further into opposition, verbal, legal and in some cases physical, to the adoption of Catholic practices within the Church of England. This is not the place for the full story of this rather sorry episode of Evangelical distraction from gospel priorities, notwithstanding the importance of maintaining Reformed doctrine within the Church of England.

Third, there was a reaction against Roman Catholicism in respect of the reassertion of both Roman dogma and territorial claims. Toleration towards Roman Catholicism increased throughout the nineteenth century. The Test and Corporation Acts (which restricted certain offices to those who received the Lord's Supper according to the usage of the Church of England) were repealed in 1828. Catholic Emancipation was further enhanced by the Catholic Relief Acts of 1829. Thus political office and the Universities of Oxford and Cambridge were now open to Catholics. There was a renewed confidence. In 1850 the re-establishment of the Roman Catholic hierarchy in England with Catholic bishops taking territorial titles was announced. This provoked a fierce Protestant and Evangelical reaction, against what was characterized as 'the papal aggression'. In 1854 the Pope declared as infallible the doctrine of the Immaculate Conception of the Blessed Virgin Mary. These events were unlikely to encourage rapprochement with Evangelical Protestants. Thus anti-Catholicism has featured as an aspect of Evangelical identity. However, this has been expressed in different ways. Positively there has been continued development of Evangelical doctrine, negatively it was expressed in ecclesiastical political action and abuse. Neither aspect can be ignored but it is the doctrinal element that forms a clearer element of Evangelical identity. Indeed, Evangelicals need to be aware that a proper concern for, for example, ecumenical relationships with Rome, or even within the Church of England, can all too easily move to a blindness to the doctrinal issues concerned.

Protestant and established: from Gorham to the 1928 Prayer Book

Evangelicals asserted both Protestant doctrine and the Protestant nature of the established Church. Although there was not a complete identity between Evangelicals and the advocacy of a political Protestantism (perhaps best characterized as 'national Protestantism'), there was considerable overlap, most especially amongst Anglican Evangelicals. The link between a Protestant state and doctrinally Protestant Anglican Evangelicals is illustrated – both positively and negatively – by two examples: the Gorham case of 1846–49 and the Prayer Book of 1928.

The case of George Cornelius Gorham is foundational for Evangelicals in the Church of England, both in terms of sacramental theology and of the long-term place for Evangelicals. The case also reveals the intricate fashion in which Protestantism has relied upon the role of the state as its final defender. The case forms part of the tussle between Evangelicals and the Oxford Movement. The Tractarians were seeking to give emphasis to a more Catholic understanding of the Prayer Book, not least in the area of the sacraments. The argument centred around baptism. Evangelicals were nervous of language which might imply that an infant was unconditionally regenerate in baptism.

In 1846 Henry Phillpotts, the High Church Bishop of Exeter, installed Gorham to the parish of St Just in Penwith. Gorham and

Phillpotts clashed over Evangelical support for a new church and an advert that Gorham placed for a curate, 'free from Tractarian error'. In August 1847 the Lord Chancellor offered Gorham the living of Brampford Speke, near Exeter. Phillpotts refused to institute Gorham until he had examined his doctrine. The examination began on 17 December 1847; it lasted five days and a further three in March 1848. Phillpotts submitted 149 questions for Gorham to answer. On 11 March 1848 Phillpotts declared Gorham to be guilty of unsound doctrine and refused to institute. The critical issue was the effect of infant baptism. The matter under formal discussion was whether or not the child in baptism was regenerate as a matter of course, with regeneration indissolubly linked to baptism. Gorham held that regeneration may be given in baptism but that it was not necessarily so. Phillpotts held that baptism was always and unconditionally effective to regeneration, or, more charitably, that lack of sin in a child meant no bar could be raised to the entry of grace. Evangelicals believed in conversion, repentance and faith; the regeneration which they sought was of the heart of the individual, baptized or not. The Book of Common Prayer referred to the child as regenerate. The question was whether or not this language was conditional, that is, conditional upon faith. Catholics pointed to the words of the liturgy. Evangelicals noted the clear conditional language of adult baptism and that the Reformed doctrine had been long held by clergy within the Church of England. Some of Gorham's supporters suspected a Catholic plot, 'popish fiction', and, probably unhelpfully, said so. A much wider group wished to maintain a breadth of interpretation, the studied ambiguity of Anglican liturgical language. If the decision against Gorham were upheld, it would be fatal for Anglican Evangelicals.

Gorham appealed to the Court of the Arches, under the Dean of the Arches, Sir Herbert Fenner Just. He found for Phillpotts. The crisis was deepening. There was no higher ecclesiastical court of appeal than the Court of the Arches. The line of appeal from here lay not to an ecclesiastical court but to the Judicial Committee of the Privy Council. Tractarians were concerned about civil courts deciding ecclesiastical cases. If Gorham were defeated, Evangelicals would secede from the Church of England. If Gorham were upheld, Tractarians would secede. The Court convened on 11 December 1849: eight laity, joined by three prelates, Canterbury, York and London. The Court found for Gorham; seven votes to one among the laity; two to one among the prelates, overall a resounding nine votes to two. They were not satisfied that this single clergyman had contradicted the formularies of the Church of England.

The second example, more briefly, concerns liturgical revision in the 1920s. Evangelicals within the Church of England were at a low ebb and in 1927 the Convocations (the gatherings of clergy representatives from the provinces of Canterbury and York) approved a revision to the Book of Common Prayer that introduced or permitted, *inter alia*, vestments, the eastward position, the wafer, the mixed chalice, reservation and adoration of the sacrament, the collect for Corpus Christi Day in the Roman Missal, Marian festivals and the Commemoration of All Souls. The Book was 'deposited' with Parliament for its approval under the 1919 Enabling Act. The provisions provoked a significant Protestant reaction led by the Church Association, whose membership grew to 100,000, and in the House of Commons by the then Home Secretary, Sir William Joynson Hicks, later 1st Viscount Brentford. The Book was rejected in the Commons by 33 votes and when reintroduced in June 1928 by an even larger 46 votes.

These examples show three things. First, they illustrate how the Anglican Evangelical position was secured within the Church of England. Second, they reveal the importance to the Anglican Evangelical constituency of the laity and third, they illustrate the link between Evangelical faith and a Protestant nation and the willingness of Evangelicals to rely, in the final resort, on the Protestant state to defend its position. This is a particular characteristic of Anglican Evangelicals due to the relationship of Church and state with the Church of England 'by law established'. On a more global scale there is no direct link between Anglicanism and the state; the Anglican Evangelical, however, will always be concerned with the Protestantism of public policy.

First-order and second-order issues

From the Reformation onwards, Protestants have sought to distinguish between issues of first importance and more secondary matters. This has been a particular characteristic of Anglican Evangelicals. Complexity arises through disagreement over what constitutes a first-order or second-order issue (the problem of definition) and the implications for fellowship and faith when first-order issues are departed from (the problem of application). The origins of the distinction between first- and second-order issues go right back into the pages of the New Testament. For example, in Acts 15 the Jerusalem Council requested restraint from Gentile believers in secondary matters. Similarly, in Romans 14, a 'weak' believer, for whom second-order issues are significant, is to be welcomed and respected. At the Reformation, Martin Luther developed the concept of *adiaphora*, things indifferent, as also in the Anglican context did Richard Hooker. In the case of the latter it was the festivals of the Church, the church calendar and certain ceremonial aspects of church life which were drawn out as examples of matters on which there could be legitimate diversity of opinion.

A first-order issue is one upon which either the basis of our *authority*, or our *salvation*, as Christians, is dependent or contingent. The basis of Christian authority is a first-order issue because it is necessary for the whole definition of Christian identity, doctrine and practice. The doctrine of salvation is a first-order issue because it effects our status before God as his people and our inheritance in heaven. Hence any issues which contradict the instruments of authority or our understanding of the person and the work of Jesus are first-order issues. Issues which would be defined in such a way would include the authority of Scripture, the deity of Jesus Christ, the incarnation, the salvific death of Christ upon the cross, the uniqueness of Christ, the work of the Holy Spirit and the return of Christ in glory to judge the living and the dead. A second-order issue is one in which a variety of opinion is permissible without contradicting either our authority or our salvation in Christ. It would include variety of practice upon which Scripture was silent (for example, presidency of the Lord's Supper), church practices such as infant or adult baptism, the mode of baptism, matters relating to vesture and issues upon which interpretative questions from Scripture may vary and which are not conditional for salvation.

Different opinions concerning biblical interpretation are not the basis of the distinction between first- and second-order issues. If that were the case there would, ultimately, be no distinction at all, every opinion carrying equal weight and all issues reduced to second order. A few guidelines are needed. Acceptance of the authority of Scripture is a starting point. Varied interpretations on issues within Scripture need (a) to give weight to the text as received (b) be consistent with other scriptural texts (c) be responsible exegesis under scriptural authority and (d) not be matters that the Bible indicates imperil salvation. More liberal traditions within the Church tend to make first-order issues second order; this is one reason for conflict and disagreement within Christianity. One example of this within the wider Anglican Church is that of presidency at the Lord's Supper. The silence of the Scriptures is interpreted narrowly as requiring presbyteral presidency. For Anglican Evangelicals scriptural silence (as on other issues) would make the issue second order and hence a variety of practice would be seen as acceptable. Both Evangelical and Catholic traditions have a tendency to make (different) second-order issues into first-order issues. This provokes dispute over non-essential issues. For Evangelicals it has traditionally been secondary matters of Church and worship which have featured in this analysis.

Anglican Evangelicals have an acute sense of the distinction between first- and second-order issues. This provides a significantly useful basis for conversation and dialogue between different traditions. The insistence of some in viewing homosexuality as second order (the issue fails all the tests for a second-order issue – see case study to follow) threatens this unity. What are the implications for fellowship and unity of disagreement over first- and second-order issues? For the Evangelical, including the Anglican Evangelical, differences over second-order issues are of no consequence for faith and fellowship. However, similarly, lack of agreement over first-order issues would constitute a denial of the faith and justify breaking fellowship, sacramental and otherwise. This illustrates two things. First, the reason for schismatic tendencies among Evangelicals when second-order issues are elevated to first order. Second, the critical importance for the long-term future of the Anglican Communion, in England and beyond, when first-order issues are breached.

Where Anglicans and Evangelicals agree and disagree

There are a number of key areas where Evangelicals and Anglicans agree and disagree. In some instances the disagreements lie over emphasis and method, especially when viewed in light of the historic position of Anglicanism. In some cases the differences are nuanced and in others more clearly delineated. There may be a variety of opinion both within and between these traditions. However, these key areas of agreement and disagreement provide both further understanding of Anglican Evangelicalism and also a basis for further conversation. The areas for debate have been characterized as five statements.

Anglicans and Evangelicals agree over the place of the Bible but disagree over the range of authority and interpretation

It might perhaps be a surprise to claim that Evangelicals and Anglicans are in agreement over the place of the Bible. However, it has been demonstrated in the preceding chapters that the essential and core beliefs of both traditions concerning the Bible are not just consistent, but shared. Failure to recognize this central shared belief and value has two significant impacts. First, it betrays the historic reality of the Anglican tradition and its foundations and formularies. Second, it prevents conversation and dialogue proceeding on the basis of an agreed core belief. Both Anglicans and Evangelicals affirm the supreme authority of Scripture in matters of both faith and practice. This is illustrated in the origins of each tradition, in canonical and liturgical expression and in devotion and practice. Thus the Thirty-Nine Articles, the Lambeth Quadrilateral, the Canons and the Declaration of Assent have demonstrated the continuity and historicity of the claim for both the centrality and the authority of the Scriptures for Anglicanism. This is reinforced in liturgical history and contemporary practice. The Bible has a significant liturgical role in Anglicanism. The public reading of the Scriptures is a central feature of Anglicanism, as is the liturgical affirmation 'this is the Word of the Lord'. Indeed, examination of the Anglican traditions of Morning and Evening Prayer reveals the reading, devotionally and liturgically, and the exposition of significant portions of Scripture. The provision by Archbishop Cranmer of the Book of Homilies was a direct response to the need to ensure whole-some and sound doctrine was encouraged. In the ordination services the giving of the Bible (or the New Testament) and its central place and importance in the ordination rites are a direct statement of both authority and purpose in ordination.

All of this is consistent with Evangelical belief about the Bible. As we have seen, Evangelicals affirm the centrality and authority of Scripture. They believe in its inspiration and in its sufficiency. Some Evangelicals express this through confessions of faith and for all Evangelicals the Bible would have a central feature in worship. Exactly like Anglicans. Well, perhaps not exactly, but certainly in a way that allows Anglican Evangelicals to be firmly rooted in the polity of both traditions. Within the Anglican tradition there is a range of views over the nature of authority, theology and biblical interpretation. Although such variety of opinion does not belong to the core of Anglicanism, it does belong to the diversity, and in certain periods the voice of this range of opinion has sometimes been louder than the core. Irrespective of the claims for the historic Anglican tradition made in this book, this heterogeneity needs to be taken seriously. The origins of the diversity derive from that line of inheritance which gives the greatest weight to the resistance to the Puritans during the reign of Elizabeth, built upon through the Caroline Divines of the seventeenth century, the liberal Anglicanism of F. D. Maurice in the nineteenth century through to more modern exponents. It is a strand of Anglican opinion in which the influence of the link to the state, the Enlightenment, the consequential advance of critical approaches to biblical interpretation and the quest for an Anglican theological method as a synthesis of various traditions are all prominent.

First, then, let us consider issues of authority. Many Anglicans will assert equivalence in authority to reason and tradition along-side Scripture. Some will pay lip service to the priority of Scripture, but only in the light of reason and tradition:

> Anglicanism is committed historically to a distinctive approach to the question of authority. Its sources of authority, dispersed as they are through many channels, are mutually restricting, mutually illuminating. In the modern intellectual situation this is beneficial, since it inhibits the enunciation of dogma, the

articulation of absolutes and the exercise of ecclesiastical authority.[8]

Thus within the wider Anglican tradition there is claim to authorities other than the Scriptures and, in some cases, weight or even equivalence is granted to them. This will lead to tensions with Evangelicals generally and Anglican Evangelicals in particular.

Second, let us consider issues of biblical interpretation and theological method. Anglicanism, or at least one strand of it, has been widely influenced by the intellectual currents dominant in each era, emphasized by the close relationship of the ecclesiastical establishment to the prevailing political order of each age. This has led to an openness to critical interpretative methods adopted under the influence of Enlightenment thought. The Bible was viewed merely as literature, and studied solely by literary method. Emphasis and weight were given to the relationships of various sources and their subsequent editing, or to the analysis of the type and genres of the biblical literature. There was more concern with the editors of Scripture, the identity of the human authors and the application of modern philosophical as well as literary presuppositions than with the divine author. The effect of this was to undermine the unity and clarity of the scriptural text. A similar process can be seen in terms of the method and approach to theology. Anglicanism has often prided itself on its scholarship and has sometimes underestimated the extent to which its scholarship has been influenced by Enlightenment rationality. Evangelicals will wish to continue to assert the transparency, clarity and power of the text of Scripture as received and also as the basis for theological reflection and investigation.

Anglicans and Evangelicals agree over the missionary imperative but disagree over the method, content and priority of the missionary enterprise

Anglicans and Evangelicals share a commitment to the spread of the gospel. This may be sometimes affected by differences in understanding and method; but the shared commitment remains. It is perhaps surprising that there should be such a synergy, but only so when Anglicanism is detached from its common roots. We have already established the global commitment of Evangelicalism as a 'catholic missionary movement', crossing cultures and denominations. The Evangelical movement has a glorious (mainly) history of missionary enterprise and endeavour. Evangelicalism has operated through both denominational and interdenominational missionary societies, through faith missions and a variety of other innovative and pioneering methods of evangelism. Evangelicals are motivated by the urgency of the gospel, its demands and power. Activism, generally, or a passion for evangelism and transformation, in particular, have characterized the Evangelical movement. The failings have tended to revolve around the export of culture rather than inculturation and sometimes a primacy given to overseas mission rather than home mission that could emphasize an imperialistic approach. Anglicanism has a similar, albeit not identical, commitment that has sometimes been lost in the midst of history. The Anglican missionary imperative has had its own characteristics and its own failings, some shared with Evangelicalism and some not. The Book of Common Prayer, in its service for the baptism of adults, recognized that there was a task of conversion for which this particular liturgical form would be useful.[9] In 1698 the oldest of the Anglican missionary societies was founded, the Society for Promoting Christian Knowledge, and in 1701 it was followed by the Society for the Propagation of the Gospel (SPG). Both these societies predate the Evangelical Revival. Clearly these early societies were closely interlinked with the development of plantations and colonies overseas: the beginnings of the Empire. The first major Anglican Evangelical society, CMS, emerged in 1799.

Anglicanism demonstrated its institutional commitment to the imperative of mission and evangelism over a long period of time. At the Edinburgh 'World Missionary Conference', in 1910, the Archbishop of Canterbury, Randall Davison, was present, alongside representatives from the SPG, CMS, the re-founded monastic societies, and leaders of nascent overseas Churches. Among others attending was William Temple. The development of the Anglican Communion (uniting Anglican Churches from around the world), William Temple's own teachings on the imperative of evangelism, successive Lambeth Conferences and the foundation of the Partnership for World Mission in 1978 have all contributed to this commitment. Most recently the commitment of Archbishop Rowan Williams and the General Synod to 'fresh expressions' and 'mission-shaped Church' have expressed in new ways the wider Anglican passion for the missionary imperative.

What are the strengths of the Anglican missionary initiatives? First, the ability of Anglicanism to generate missionary endeavour across the breadth of its traditions. Second, the institutional commitment of Anglicanism to world mission. Third, the strength, and depth, of the commitment of the visible Church to mission. Fourth, a flexibility, usually, that allowed Anglicanism to be adaptable to changing context and circumstances. What then were the weaknesses? First, the exporting of Anglicanism rather than the gospel. To some extent this was also a characteristic of the Anglican Evangelical missionary societies although this was balanced by the wider Evangelical movement. Anglican mission, however, from whichever tradition or source, tended to include the export of episcopal government and common prayer as well as the gospel. Second, Anglican mission was closely associated with 'imperial power', it was not just Anglicanism that was being exported, but English culture. Third, this led to a lack of flexibility when it came to working across denominational divides. Fourth, the swift ability of Anglicanism to associate with civic society and civil power gave an aura of respectability, but excluded many from the reach of the gospel.

On occasion, both historically and in the contemporary world, this passion and commitment have been either obscured over debate concerning the content of the gospel to be shared or enveloped in the culture of society. The tensions between Evangelical and Anglican arise over the relative place of the institutional methods of evangelism, perceived weight given to Anglican forms of church polity alongside the essence of the gospel and associated inflexibility in working with other Christians. However, the shared commitment to the gospel, with many shared strengths and weaknesses in its propagation, gives Anglicans and Evangelicals both a common value and a platform for conversation.

Anglicans and Evangelicals agree over ecumenical and global commitment but disagree over content and method

There is a shared commitment of Anglicanism and Evangelicalism to ecumenical progress and dialogue, though expressed in differing ways. If the suggestion that a shared commitment to the imperative of mission might be surprising from the Anglican perspective (but has been shown not to be), then that of shared enthusiasm for ecumenism might be seen as surprising from the Evangelical perspective. However, once again, appreciation of the story so far illustrates this not to be so.

Anglican theology has long affirmed the Anglican Church as part of the universal, holy and apostolic Church. Anglicanism has always given weight to the biblical imperative for unity and not seen itself as the only true expression of Church (though it has acted, and continues sometimes to act as though it does). Unity is an important objective for Anglicanism. The Anglican ecumenical endeavour has a number of strengths. First, the commitment is institutionally strong; there is an explicit priority and desire to work with other Christian Churches, to work at differences, to talk and to have dialogue. Second, ecumenical dialogue includes Rome and other institutional Protestant Churches. There is thus a breadth to the dialogue. As most strengths have a corresponding weakness, so this breadth can also be seen as narrow in terms of today's Christianity. Third, there is a concentration on things in common. The areas of agreement are emphasized rather than areas of disagreement. We have seen that catholicity lies at the heart of Evangelicalism. Thus there is a ready-made ecumenical movement, united in the essential truths of the gospel, already expressing that unity which the wider Anglican tradition seeks. The Evangelical commitment also has its significant strengths. First, the priority of the essentials of the gospel. Second, the importance of truth as a basis for unity. Third, the experience and practical commitment to working together in the cause of the gospel.

What are the weaknesses of the Anglican approach and how can tensions arise? First, there is a priority given to visible, even institutional unity, rather than unity in the truth of the gospel. Truth and unity belong together but sometimes are separated due to the differing weight accorded to each by Evangelical and Anglican traditions respectively.

Second, agreement tends to be at the level of lowest common denominator. The ecumenical method adopted in modern Anglicanism is that of the 'common statement'. This approach has been used in much contemporary ecumenical dialogue. Common statements have been produced in recent years in respect of relationships with the German Protestant Church (the EKD) – the Meissen Common Statement, the Scandinavian Churches – the Porvoo Common Statement and the French Protestant Church – the Reuilly Declaration. The approach has been similar in the development of the Methodist Covenant and also in respect of ARCIC (the Anglican–Roman Catholic International Commission). The problem for Evangelicals is rarely with what is agreed in the common statement but what is excluded or assumed. Hence, in the talks with the Methodist Church the failure to recognize the importance of the doctrinal differences between the two traditions as well as an assertion of episcopacy and priesthood which went beyond the received Anglican tradition caused many Anglican Evangelicals considerable disquiet in what might have seemed on the face of it a rather obvious ecumenical endeavour.

Third, there is an overemphasis on unity with Rome (at least in modern Anglicanism) and institutional Protestantism rather than new, emerging and growing expressions of church life, those very Churches which are both rapidly growing and natural partners (at least in some respects) for Evangelicals. Globally this would include both classic and newer expressions of Pentecostalism and, in the UK, the 'new Churches', black Churches and other Evangelical Churches. The problem for the Anglican Evangelical in the talks with Rome is not that dialogue is inappropriate, but that the emphasis in one particular direction sits ill at ease with the doctrinal understanding of historic Anglicanism. Hence, documents dealing with the doctrine of the Eucharist, the place of Mary and the role of a universal primate have not only been presented as either 'agreed' or at least agreed by the necessary body itself, but generated much dissent amongst Anglican Evangelicals.

Fourth, sometimes the voice of only one particular tradition of Anglicanism is heard; and that is rarely the Evangelical voice of any particular description. If 'middle Anglicanism' talks to 'liberal Protestantism', or 'Catholic Anglicanism' talks to Rome, then an illusion of unity may be gained. In ecumenical dialogue tension arises between Anglican and Evangelical when the former fails to acknowledge or give weight to the historic tradition of Anglicanism or when that tradition and its contemporary exponents are marginalized. Sometimes it is only in debate in the General Synod that ecumenical partners come to recognize the diversity of opinion within the Anglican tradition.

Evangelicalism, too, has its weaknesses in approach. First, commitment to unity in the gospel has sometimes been expressed more in theory than in practice. Second, Evangelicals have sometimes sought unity on the basis of second-order issues not essential for salvation. Third, Evangelicals have on occasion underplayed the importance of visible unity. In spite of all of this, Evangelicals and Anglicans share a common commitment to Christian unity, upon which further dialogue and conversation can be built. Perhaps the increased prominence and role of the Anglican Communion might be a considerable building block towards this dialogue.

Anglicans and Evangelicals agree on the importance of engaging society but disagree over where the priority of transformation lies

This claim, too, may seem surprising to some. However, historically both Anglicans and Evangelicals have asserted the importance and significance of the gospel for wider society. Both traditions have given practical expression to this commitment and both have also, on occasion, displayed failings; in the case of the Anglican, in submerging under society, and in the case of the Evangelical in withdrawing from society. Anglicanism is drawn to engagement with society. It brings a commitment to valuing all people as created in God's image, a concern for the wholeness of society, a recognition of the responsibilities of leadership and governance, and, at least in the Church of England, a territorial commitment to the care for all people. These are powerful influences in support of the gospel. The complexities for Anglicanism have arisen when engagement has become more important than transformation. Hence Anglicanism can be susceptible to the claims of status, power and influence that blunt the message of the gospel. Similarly, Anglicanism can sometimes confuse the gospel message with a political one. That is not to suggest that the gospel does not have political implications; rather that sometimes the political rationale for change can be seen as taking a priority over the gospel's imperative for change.

For the Evangelical movement it can sometimes be thought that there is a lack of engagement with society. Clearly there have been instances when this has been the case. Historically, however, Evangelicals have been committed to the transformation of society. The strengths of the movement lie in the urgency and activism of the gospel for society and the passionate concern for change. Tensions for the movement arise in assessing or debating the relative priorities of personal conversion or social change in society. Tensions can emerge between Anglican and Evangelical traditions over where the priority of transformation lies and the methodology of approach. The former will tend to emphasize and give weight to the transforming power of the gospel on the structures of society. This will be seen in political comment and action, both in the context of the debate of ideas and ideology, but also in the practical application of governmental policy. In this context the role of the voluntary Christian agency and the importance of individual conversion can be lost. Similarly, the potency of Anglican polity for change can become submerged within society and culture rather than presenting a challenge for change and transformation. An example of this would be continued debate over the place of Church schools, both in principle but also in terms of their distinctiveness. However, the common commitment to change should act to bring Evangelicals and Anglicans together. The combination of emphases should be seen as powerful motives and influences for change. Both traditions bring significant opportunities and commitments. However, if the dialogue is to be fruitful, it also requires honest assessment of the differences in approach. This whole area of relationship will be fully explored in Chapter 4.

Anglicans and Evangelicals agree over the importance of the Church, but disagree over the priority of the visible Church

It is perhaps in the understanding of the place of the Church that Anglican Evangelicals find the greatest tension between first- and second-order issues and also with wider Anglicanism. The debate is concerned with *ecclesiology* (the doctrine of the Church). Anglican Evangelicals draw their basic understanding of the Church firstly from the pages of the New Testament and secondly from the Thirty-Nine Articles. Key to Anglican Evangelical ecclesiology is the recognition that a detailed blueprint is not laid down. However, we do have the picture of Acts 2.42–47, a dynamic view of the primitive Church which emphasizes apostolic teaching, prayer, worship and the breaking of bread. This is much appealed to by those most influenced by the Charismatic tradition as it may represent one of the earliest pictures of the primitive Church. The Pastoral Epistles, written much later, give a picture of a more organized, structured, institutional Church. From these sources the Anglican Church has drawn its offices of deacon, presbyter and bishop. However, both in the Pastorals and in Acts 20 the word for overseer or bishop (*episkopos*) and the word for elder or presbyter (*presbyteros*) are used interchangeably. Hence for the Anglican Evangelical the relationship between deacon, presbyter and bishop as three orders of ministry is less clear-cut than for some others within the Anglican Church. Anglican Evangelicals recognize the importance of a wider ministry of oversight but base the rationale for it more on Paul's commissioning of Timothy and Titus than from formal offices laid down in Scripture. In summary, then, Anglican Evangelicals view the role of bishop as a pragmatic form of good church government consistent with the Scriptures, rather than as an essential component of the Church. This is characterized as the bishop being of the *bene esse* (well-being) of the Church, rather than of the *esse* (being or very essence) of the Church. This can, both historically and in the contemporary Anglican Church, lead to tension.

Article 19 describes the visible Church as 'a congregation of faithful men, in which the pure Word of God is preached, and the Sacraments be duly administered according to Christ's ordinance ...' The question, therefore, is raised of the relationship between the visible and invisible Church and to what extent the one should resemble the other. The Anglican Evangelical will generally expect the visible Church first, to resemble Article 19, and second, at least to approximate to the invisible. Thus boundaries of doctrine and behaviour will be expected. The Anglican Evangelical will be motivated by the maxim *ecclesia semper reformanda est* – the Church always needs to be reformed. To the extent that the Anglican weighs the priority of the visible Church, perhaps even to the extent of a lack of boundary or discipline or holiness, then there will be tension with the Anglican Evangelical. In short, Anglicans who are not Evangelicals tend to give a priority to the visible Church, while Evangelicals will prioritize the invisible Church. As will be seen from the case study later, this has direct implications for the Anglican Evangelical understanding of Church and ministry and its contemporary application.

Case Studies

Human Sexuality

Why is it impossible to write a book concerned with Anglican Evangelicalism without mentioning human sexuality? The answer is not as straightforward as it might seem. Sexuality seems to prevail in the Church's agenda. There again, the subject also dominates much of cultural and political life. Debate over civil partnerships is cultural and political as well as theological. Inevitably, therefore, church discussion is not only theological debate, but also a reflection of wider cultural themes. This case study is not a further debate about biblical or other arguments concerned with sexuality. It is not an exposition of a case – any case. Rather, the purpose is to draw out the underlying theological issues, and then to reflect on how Anglican Evangelicalism responds to these issues and hence what particular contribution to the wider debate can come from this constituency.

Some background is necessary. Historians love the clarity of dates to mark movements and events. The reality is more complex. The debates over human sexuality in the Church have been taking place over many years, partly in response to the wider cultural agenda, with theological writing on both sides of the debate. Two events, early in the twenty-first century, brought matters to a head in terms of the polity of the Anglican Church. Unsurprisingly, both these events occurred in the northern hemisphere, one in England and one in the USA, both areas of long-term decline of Anglican Christian witness. The first was the nomination of Canon Jeffrey John, to the Suffragan See of Reading. Canon John had written and taught on the admissibility of homosexual practice within the life of the Church. He was also, by his own account, homosexual and in a now celibate partnership. This is not the place for the detailed story of the events. Suffice it to say that the nomination was challenged, and Canon John withdrew his acceptance following meetings with the Archbishop of Canterbury. In the midst of this particular controversy the second event arose in the USA. In this instance Canon Vicky Gene Robinson was nominated, and subsequently confirmed, as Bishop of New Hampshire. Canon Robinson, divorced from his wife, was and is in an active homosexual partnership of many years standing. A number of issues arose from these two events and subsequent developments.

- The nature of authority within Anglicanism
- The content of biblical teaching
- The nature of leadership within the Church
- The implications for the Anglican Communion (catholicity)

In the debates surrounding these events these critical underlying issues have often become disguised due to concern with the details. The issue of authority is crucial. It is a prior issue to that of the content of the authority. The debates over sexuality tend to be fought on two levels. First, the autonomy of human experience (for example, the intensity of experience of the love of God in a same-sex union) or rationality (concepts of equality in society). Second, discussion over what constitutes the teaching of the Bible. It could not be clearer from the discussion so far that for the faithful Anglican Evangelical the determinative authority is Scripture.

Let us also consider the issue of scriptural interpretation. It is important in all of these discussions to assess at once whether the debate is about the nature of authority or the content of an agreed authority. The Anglican Evangelical will always wish to work hard at scriptural teaching on the matter of sexuality, including an openness to change (or else the concept of authority becomes meaningless). Similarly the Anglican Evangelical will wish to allow the clarity of the biblical text to speak. It is manifestly the case that the entire trajectory of biblical teaching in respect of homosexual practice is negative. Care, however, is needed. It is, for example, significantly less clear that the Bible distinguishes on the basis of orientation as opposed to practice. Such a distinction is a much more modern concept. However, it is also the case that the Bible does not teach moral equivalence between a variety of different lifestyle options. To these debates the Anglican Evangelical will be particularly attuned.

When it comes to the nature of leadership, the Anglican Evangelical will also have a distinctive line, drawn from the Scriptures. In the debates over the appointment of Canon John as Bishop of Reading and that of Canon Robinson to New Hampshire, there was an important difference. In the latter case there was a clear issue of a lifestyle and its compatibility with Scripture. In the former, although there were lifestyle questions, that was not the central issue. What was at the heart of the matter there was the written, public advocacy of teaching which was seen as incompatible with that of Scripture. This matter was emphasized in the light of the teaching of the New Testament concerning the nature of leadership and oversight. The office of bishop or overseer involves particular responsibility for teaching, indeed the teaching of sound doctrine and refutation of false teaching. The office is an important factor in the transmission of 'the faith once received by the saints'. Again on the basis of the authority of Scripture the Anglican Evangelical will have a particular view of leadership, its nature and its responsibilities, an important feature of this debate.

Finally, the issue of Communion and catholicity. The implications of the issues of human sexuality have raised particular questions about the nature of the Anglican Communion. Hence the matters under debate have global and catholic implications. It raises the question of whether the Anglican Communion is linked together either doctrinally ('a common faith') or sociologically ('a common family') together with the nature and boundaries of any such Communion. The situation in the USA is given more weight due to the long-term departure of ECUSA and its triennial General Convention from the traditional biblical faith of Anglicanism in favour of a liberal Protestantism in wider matters of Trinitarian doctrine and Christology. So when in 2006 the newly-elected Presiding Bishop, Katharine Jefferts Schori, preached her first sermon, she referred to 'Our mother Jesus gives birth to a new creation . . .'[10] Most Evangelicals and biblical Christians would reply that Jesus is our Lord and Saviour and in him we are new creations. The distinctions are very important.

Anglican Evangelicals will be particularly keen to ensure that they are not stripped of their catholicity. That catholicity should act as a restraint on either precipitate action or on removing a member of the family. The restraint to be exercised, however, is not conclusive. Anglican Evangelicalism will wish to contribute to the debate concerning boundaries with observations that there are indeed boundaries that require discipline as well as generosity, and that doctrine defines the limits of the common faith. It is important that sex, sexuality or homosexuality are not, as such, the defining characteristics of any boundaries. Rather, the limits must be defined in terms of departure in matters of faith of the first order.

Where does this leave us in the case study on human sexuality? Three concluding comments will suffice. First, human sexuality is symptom rather than first cause. The issues and debates derive from the underlying issues of authority and the nature of leadership within the Church. For those who view sexuality as a second-order issue, it is important to recognize that the underlying questions are all of the first order. The issues are lifestyle and teaching which contradict the Scriptures. Second, the Church does have boundaries, doctrinal limits, which require discipline. Third, the catholicity of the Church requires adherence to a common faith, and neither our Evangelical doctrine nor our global catholicity should be surrendered for practices – sexual, behavioural or doctrinal – which lie outside that common faith of Anglicanism. Anglican Evangelicalism will wish to engage deeply, biblically, generously and globally in order to strengthen the convictions of Anglicanism and the Anglican Communion.

Church, ministry and sacraments

Robert Runcie challenged Anglican Evangelicals at their National Congress in 1987 over ecclesiology. Evangelicals needed a more developed doctrine of the Church, to renew, clarify and broaden their ecclesiology. He called upon Evangelicals to integrate more fully and view the Church of England as more than a convenient ship. He was given a standing ovation. Ecclesiology is the doctrine of the Church. It includes an understanding of the Church and its nature, its worship, ministry and sacraments. The critique that Anglican Evangelicals lack a coherent ecclesiology has been urged repeatedly both before and since Runcie's comments from both within and without the movement. Anglican Evangelicals have tended to respond with an embarrassed silence. The presumption is made that Evangelicals have no ecclesiology or that it is inadequate. The claim is usually made by those who adopt very particular ecclesiological positions, understandings which display equally, if not deeper, inadequate ecclesiologies. Sometimes, in debate, ecclesiology is used by those with a particularly developed – perhaps overdeveloped – sense of the priority of the visible Church, as a conversation stopper or idea killer. Anglican Evangelicals most certainly do have an ecclesiology. The applause for the Archbishop in 1987 certainly exposed the fact that many Anglican Evangelicals had an inadequate understanding of their own heritage. It also made manifest the way in which the

ecclesiological heritage of the Church of England and of Anglicanism has indeed become disguised. What *is* inadequate is what passes
for ecclesiology in much of the modern Church of England. What
is also inadequate is the manner in which this has become so
detached from the foundations of Anglicanism. There are a
number of areas where the Anglican Evangelical understanding of
ministry comes into conflict with what passes for modern, middle
Anglican ecclesiology. These include the following:

• The role and nature of episcopacy
• The understanding of the teaching role of the presbyterate
• The nature of the local church as the prime unit of ministry
• Understanding, nature and frequency of the Lord's Supper

For the purposes of this case study we are going to consider two
particular areas of tension for Anglican Evangelicals, eucharistic
presidency and church planting. These two examples illustrate in
both theory and practice why ecclesiology generates tension, but
seek also to place these questions in both historical and contemporary context.

Eucharistic presidency
Who may preside at the celebration of the Lord's Supper? The
answer depends upon the ecclesiological presumptions which are
in place. The response is affected by a number of factors:

• The teaching of Scripture on the Supper, Ministry and Church
• The nature of the Supper
• Church order

We have seen that the Anglican Evangelical understanding of
ministry drawn from Scripture gives weight to teaching, locality,
preaching and oversight. Scripturally the ordained ministry is not
linked to the Lord's Supper or Holy Communion. The 'breaking
of bread' is associated in the Bible with the Last Supper at which
Jesus shared bread and wine with his disciples, and which is most
likely (though not all the evidence points to this, not least issues
of calendar and chronology in John's gospel) with the Passover. It
was evidently a feature of life in the early Church, as shown by
both Acts and 1 Corinthians, although not without controversy.

Scripture makes no comment on who may preside at a celebration of Communion. Interestingly, this fact is acknowledged by the Report of the House of Bishops of the Church of England into eucharistic presidency:

> However, as far as eucharistic presidency is concerned, there is no indication anywhere in the New Testament of an explicit link between the Church's office and presiding at the Eucharist.[11]
> There is no suggestion that anyone was ordained or appointed to an office which constituted primarily of saying the blessing over the bread and wine.[12]

In a way rather inconsistent with the historic Anglican tradition this official report then draws its conclusion from silence in a manner that demeans the authority of Scripture.

> It would therefore be a mistake to jump from the silence of these severely limited sources to the conclusion that the eucharistic presidency was, in principle, open to anyone.[13]

One quite explicit Anglican characteristic, advocated by all traditions in the Church and clearly set forth by Richard Hooker, is that if Scripture is silent then a variety of practice is permitted. That is the justification for various aspects of liturgical form and celebration. Similarly, to describe the source of Scripture as 'severely limited' risks undermining the common authoritative source for the faith, life and practice of the Church. The scriptural silence explains why Evangelicals in principle support lay presidency at the Lord's Table.

The Anglican understanding of the Supper, as set out in the Articles and Prayer Books, is that of a memorial, centred on the once for all sacrificial death of Christ, effective through the faithful reception of the bread and wine. Clearly this understanding of the Communion requires no particular emphasis either upon consecration or upon the qualifications of those consecrating. That is not to say that differing traditions and understandings of Communion have not developed within the Anglican tradition; simply that such alternatives are not consistent with the historic foundations. Thus a more developed or 'Catholic' understanding of the Eucharist will clearly lead to greater restrictions upon who may preside and this then connects to a more sacerdotal understanding of the ministry, its order and function.

Finally, church order. This is an important area for Anglicanism (recalling Bishop Jewel's defence of the Reformation settlement in England) and explains why some Evangelicals resist lay presidency. However, those Evangelicals have been largely influenced, in those circumstances, by a Catholic argument. In essence the argument of the House of Bishops was based upon appeal to church order (since they agreed that Scripture was silent). The unity and order of the Church and ministry requires, so the argument would advance, Catholic order. In other words ministry must be properly authorized through episcopal ordination, have regard for the universality of the ministry, not act contrary to the wider Church and be for good order. However, these same arguments did not prevent the admission of women to the presbyterate (contrary to at least some aspects of Catholic order). In addition, order would require unity between Word and Sacrament (a cherished Anglican couplet) and since the laity are permitted to preach, there can be no good argument for preventing the laity – or at least authorized laity – from presiding at the Communion.

Historically, Anglican Evangelicals have proved flexible over church order in the interests of the gospel. Examples have included a shortage of human agents at home or overseas (lay ministry and the role of female missionaries in the nineteenth century) or the need to take the gospel to those who have not heard (whether in industrial England or overseas colonies or elsewhere). Order remains important, but as has been illustrated, reliance on church order for the argument will simply lead to debates over the differing nature and practice of order. Evangelicals, characteristically, will always prefer the scriptural arguments, not least when supported by the traditional and historic Anglican approaches to matters on which Scripture is not prescriptive.

Church planting

Church planting is a relatively modern term; as a practice it is as old as the apostolic testimony. It is an area of church life which has led to tension within Anglicanism and even between Anglican Evangelicals. Church planting is inextricably linked to the evangelistic, missionary understanding of the Church. It may take place in a number of ways:

- The planting of a separate congregation within the same church family
- The establishment of a separate congregation within the same parish
- The establishment of a separate congregation outside the same parish
- The grafting of a group into or onto an existing congregation outside the parish

The issues of polity which are raised are as follows:

- The sacrosanct nature of the parochial system
- The role of the bishop
- The provision of ministry for the planted congregation

These are all matters of church order. Insofar as the local congregation and bishop are able to cooperate and agree, then whichever model is adopted and whatever provision is made can proceed. The complexity, difficulty and sometimes tension can arise when there is no such agreement. This usually arises if the new congregation is to be established outside the existing parochial boundaries and sometimes extends into how ministry is to be provided. The Anglican Evangelical will always proceed in good order and cooperation, but if agreement is unreasonably denied, then the apostolic imperative will take priority even if that leads to conflict with others.

The most recent celebrated case concerned church planting in the Diocese of Southwark in 2006. The matter was complicated by being linked, fairly or not, to the Bishop of Southwark's acceptance of the House of Bishops' statement on civil partnerships. The case generated heat both within and without Anglican Evangelicalism. The Revd Richard Coekin was responsible for a number of church plants which had been originally established from Emmanuel, Wimbledon (to which he was licensed), an Anglican proprietary chapel (hence outside the jurisdiction of the Bishop in respect of appointments and stipends, but not in respect of licensing and oaths of obedience). There was clearly strain within the diocese over both the stance of the Bishop on civil partnerships and on the appropriateness of the plants concerned. Relationships had broken down. The question which faced the leadership of the church plants was how to provide for ongoing ordained leadership and ministry. After the breakdown of negotiations over the possible ordination of three trained personnel from within the churches, a bishop from the Church of England in South Africa (a Church not in communion with the Church of England) ordained the men concerned in an Anglican parish church. Richard Coekin's licence was withdrawn by the Bishop. He appealed to the Archbishop of Canterbury and won his appeal for restoration of licence.

The outcome of the case is instructive. Richard Coekin was deemed to have been worthy of censure for his part in organizing the alternative ordinations, though the only ecclesiastical offence to have been committed was the provision of an Anglican parish church for a non-Anglican ordination. There were two judgments. First, the process followed by the bishop was deemed seriously flawed. Second, the decision to withdraw the licence was considered inappropriate. The licence was restored on the usual terms (ignoring the advice of the bishop who presided over the appeal hearing that specific undertakings should be sought) – these terms of course include the acceptance of episcopal authority within its normal boundaries. Those ordained were now ordained ministers of the Church of England in South Africa and not authorized to function in the Church of England – a fact not in dispute. The report of the case referred to the Trust Deed of Dundonald Church (the church plant concerned) and noted its normal requirement for the minister to be an ordained Anglican and licensed by the appropriate bishop. It was noted that although the church operated outside the official structures of the diocese it sought to maintain an essentially Anglican ethos, reinforced by the appellant's position as Assistant Minister of Emmanuel, Wimbledon and supported explicitly by the incumbent of that church.[14]

It is not intended here to comment on the merits or otherwise of this case or its consequences. Rather, the purpose is to draw attention to the relationship of apostolic church planting and church order. Essential to understanding this case is the priority of the local church in terms of Anglican definition and ministry. Certainly church order and episcopal oversight was to be provided (and accepted), but the defining characteristics of the church's Anglican identity were its trust deed, ethos and link to another Anglican parish church. Anglican polity most certainly involved oversight, but was not to be defined in relation to a diocese and its structure. Hence, Anglican Evangelicals will be encouraged by this decision (not all were – some preferred the approach of definition by diocese and bishop) because it gives some weight to the historic understanding of Anglicanism, encourages the apostolic ministry of church planting and maintains an important role for episcopal oversight; but not an unlimited one. The problems of ministry and ordination and the implications for church order are well illustrated by the case, if not entirely resolved in a satisfactory manner within the polity of the Anglican Church.

Assessment: the self-understanding of Anglican Evangelicals for the future

Anglican Evangelicalism and its relationships to the wider movements have been described and analysed with regard to both cohesion and tension. The question remains, however, of the critical self-understanding of the Anglican Evangelical tradition, the challenges it faces and its future prospects.

Nature of Anglican Evangelicalism

It would be tempting to regard Anglican Evangelicalism as a moderate form of the Evangelical tradition, tolerated as part of the Anglican family, but not really belonging. This would fail to do justice to each of these traditions, with all of their strengths and weaknesses. It might also be convenient to regard Anglican Evangelicalism as purely an English phenomenon. However, that would ignore the global catholicity of the movement. Rather, Anglican Evangelicalism is a manifestation of the Christian faith which gives fullness of expression to the core foundational beliefs of both Anglican and Evangelical Christian traditions. In doing so, each informs the other. The particular power of the Evangelical influence on Anglicanism has been to empower, enliven and renew the historic Reformed Anglican faith.

The Anglican Evangelical tradition is thus both Reformed and renewed. Theologically and historically it represents a moderate Calvinism that successfully holds together the Reformed doctrinal heritage of Anglicanism with the Evangelical spiritual heritage of conversion and evangelism. Theologically also it holds the long-standing developed Anglican emphasis on the incarnation in creative tension with the atonement, giving a potentially extremely powerful new dynamic to being both counter-cultural and culturally engaged. The substitutionary atonement is central, and the cross demands a response both individually and corporately. Liturgically, it has traditionally represented the doctrinal conservatism of the Book of Common Prayer – drawing both intellectually and emotionally upon the 1552 book – but this has weakened in favour of more contemporary worship, not least under the influence of Charismatic renewal. The place of the Bible is central, bringing emphasis upon the authority of Scripture and its essential clarity, but also the need for interpretation and scholarly understanding. The hard work of reading the text, understanding and interpreting that text faithfully, is a characteristic of the tradition. However, it is the received text of the Scriptures that remains determinative. Anglican Evangelicalism also brings a willingness, perhaps one might say a greater willingness than the wider Evangelical tradition, to weigh properly first- and second-order issues. Anglican Evangelicalism is not, however, willing to reduce first-order matters of faith and salvation to matters of second-order equivalence.

Anglican Evangelicalism embraces the episcopal form of church government. It does not invest the form of oversight with the same degree of authority as the essential content or nature of the oversight, that of ensuring continuity of doctrinal orthodoxy in line with the faith once delivered to the saints. This, once again, provides a dynamic for Anglican Evangelicalism in terms of the renewal of leadership within the Church. Its view of ministry is flexible and dynamic, with much emphasis upon lay leadership. The episcopal role is one of accountability and oversight. This same flexibility is shown in respect of church order. The tensions that can sometimes arise have been noted in the case studies; however, the power of the Anglican Evangelical tradition lies in its ability to be flexible, risk-taking and wide-ranging in its scope for the sake of the gospel.

Contemporary challenges

What then are the challenges to this picture of Anglican Evangelicalism? A major challenge to Anglican Evangelicalism is the loss of historical perspective and hence of corporate memory. The implications of this loss have been heightened, in some respects, by the impact of Charismatic renewal. This loss of perspective and insight lessens the corporate knowledge of the nature and identity of Anglican Evangelicalism. It reduces both its distinctive contribution and its ability to contribute to dynamic conversation within Anglicanism. It permits some Evangelicals, and others within the Anglican tradition, to acquiesce in seeing Evangelicals as not really belonging. Hence some Evangelicals reduce Anglicanism to 'the best boat to fish from', and some other Anglicans exclude Evangelicals as 'not really Anglican'. Both are inadequate responses. This loss of memory of the tradition is illustrated in two ways. The first is the decline of understanding of the nature and place of the Anglican formularies. As has been shown, the Book of Common Prayer (and its origins), the Thirty-Nine Articles and the Ordinal are essential elements in Anglican Evangelical self-understanding. The second is the separation of Word and Spirit. Hence it can be suggested that new revelations of God are brought about separate from the revealed Word. This can have a particularly devastating impact in embracing new fashionable trends in church life as 'illuminations of the Spirit', without reference to sound doctrine as revealed in Scripture.

The Charismatic movement has brought much new and renewed life to Anglican Evangelicals. Indeed the ability of Anglicanism to accommodate spiritual renewal movements is impressive. However, it is imperative that Word (God's self-revelation in Christ through his written Word) and Spirit (God's current action both in the heart of the believer in relationship with him and more widely) are held together. If not, then there will be no objective revelation by which to discern spiritual illumination and insight. In that case unscriptural innovations become invested and baptized with the Holy Spirit. The fresh action of the Spirit was invoked significantly at the General Convention of ECUSA in June 2006 to justify same-sex unions and other unbiblical practices.

One of the outcomes of Charismatic renewal has been the renewal of worship. In many cases this has led to greater informality of Anglican worship, perhaps also greater variety. It is too simplistic to reduce this phenomenon to a rejection of liturgical forms of worship, but in weekly parish life it is often manifested in such a way. Contemporary worship is likely to continue to be a significant factor in Anglican Evangelicalism. However, alongside this shift has been a loss of not just the form of the Book of Common Prayer and its antecedents, but also of its nature, theology and content. This trend, the lack of understanding and appreciation of the nature, content and purpose of the Prayer Books needs to be reversed in order for Anglican Evangelical self-understanding not just to be preserved, but to be enhanced alongside Charismatic renewal. A further challenge from within is the tendency to build tradition rather than challenge or renew tradition. Anglican Evangelicals face cultural, institutional and experiential pressure to build and establish subcultures and traditions from both sides of the heritage they claim. It may indeed be a strength of Anglican Evangelicalism that it understands the distinction of first- and second-order issues and that it refuses to treat first order as second order. However, it can easily slip into the trap of elevating second-order issues to first order.

Two brief examples will suffice. First, the anti-Catholic tendency within Anglican Evangelicalism has already been noted. That strand cannot be ignored; it is seen in the Thirty-Nine Articles and was an important factor in identity in the Anglican Evangelicalism of the nineteenth century. However, this aspect of the tradition can sometimes move, perhaps too easily, from a proper concern for Reformed doctrine to a cultural anti-Catholicism. Although this has been seen in Northern Ireland in its most extreme forms, it can lead to reluctance to work with others both within and without the Church – thus negating Evangelical catholicity. It is expressed in an unhealthy obsession with opposing the form, style and symbol of the Catholic tradition. Anglican Evangelicalism must keep focused upon essential matters of faith and mission. Second, there is the tendency to private judgement in matters of church order. Particular styles, dress (or lack of it), righteousness of judgement – perhaps even self-righteousness – unwillingness to consult or accept accountability of relationships with those in oversight, are all elements of church order which if elevated to matters of first importance will both distract and distort Anglican Evangelicalism. There may be good reason for elements of these aspects of identity and characteristics of the tradition to feature as part of our life but not its centre. Similarly the charge that Anglican Evangelicals lack an ecclesiology is both an unworthy and unwarranted assertion – ever more so if Anglican Evangelicals work, as is suggested subsequently, in building up the global catholicity of the movement. However, if Anglican Evangelicalism places too much weight on the particulars of its own ecclesiastical subculture, it will lose both the humility of its Lord and the opportunity for transformation.

A final challenge to note is the danger of loss of urgency in the mission of the gospel. This is reinforced by the ever-present tendency to institutionalization within the tradition. Evangelicals who assume episcopal office are often (though not always) viewed with disappointment by the wider tradition, not because they properly seek to ensure they serve the whole Church, but because they sometimes seem to place the form of the institution and the trappings of establishment above the urgency of the gospel. This is no less an error than the Evangelical elevation of their own particular matters of church order. Wider Anglican polity contributes to this lack of urgency through a centralized and unwieldy financial system that is a disincentive to growth, an overemphasis on the occasional offices, an unhealthy interest in titles, positions and promotions and a lack of clarity over the essentials of the gospel. This sometimes extends to an unwillingness to embrace, or even allow, creative approaches to church, church planting and church growth. Evangelicals contribute in their own unhealthy interests and obsessions already referred to, together with their own loss of confidence in some respects in the revelation in Scripture and the power of the saving grace of the gospel. The urgency of the gospel needs to be the clarion call of Anglican Evangelicalism.[15]

Future prospects

In this assessment, and ever aware of the weaknesses as well as the strengths of the tradition, let us consider five aspects of future prospects for this particular form of Reformed Christianity.

First, the *reclaiming* of authority. Where does authority lie and our confidence in that authority? For the Christian, for whom the biblical witness is determinative, the characteristics of any authority must be on the basis of God's divinity and God's initiative. In other words, *revelation* is central. The long-term drift of the institutional Protestant Churches into theological liberalism is explained in part by a loss of confidence in revelation. Hedonism (the pursuit of pleasure), moral equivalence (equating of moral ideas on the basis of human reason or experience) and self-centredness are, in the global context in which we live, exposed for all their inadequacies. The epoch-changing rediscovery by Luther of God's righteousness, and initiative in faith, reclaimed authority for God's *grace*, God's *initiative* and God's *Word*. We need a new Reformation, to transform both society and Church. How does God reveal himself? Supremely in the person of Jesus, but also uniquely and authoritatively in Holy Scripture through whom Jesus Christ is made known and through which we hear God speak to us today. Listening must always involve first listening to God. The opportunity is that despite crisis and division there is a hunger for the Bible as the bankruptcy of Western culture leaves an enormous vacuum. Into the void, God spoke. Anglican Evangelicalism is well placed to bring about this reclaiming of the nature of authority. Both its key traditions affirm the authority of the Scriptures. Anglican Evangelicalism provides a clarity yet also a context for interpretation. It is distinguished from a crude fundamentalism, it provides an ecclesiological tradition, an awareness of first- and second-order issues and an opportunity for the wider Anglican tradition to recover its emphasis upon revelation. This will not go unchallenged from both within and without the Church. We will see this expressed in the next decade over the uniqueness of Jesus. Anglican Evangelicalism needs to turn its many strengths to this particular topic, to work at and deepen our understanding of Jesus and his uniqueness in preparation for the challenges to come.

Second, the *rediscovery* of identity. Yes, a variety of Christian traditions have arisen within Anglicanism. However, historical perspective recognizes that Anglican Evangelicalism is the tradition which represents the greatest continuity from the foundation of the Anglican Church. Anglican Evangelicalism needs to rediscover its identity. Is this simply a plea to be more Protestant or more Reformed or more Evangelical? More, it is a plea to recognize the whole basis of Anglicanism as an expression of Christianity based clearly and squarely upon the authority of Scripture. It is around the Bible that we coalesce. Yes, we need the doctrinal formularies, but also the impact of Evangelical renewal and the centrality of the relationship with Jesus at the heart of our spirituality. Spiritual renewal is desperately needed – a rediscovery of roots and identity can both feed and be fed by such renewal.

The gift of the Bible, of the priesthood of all, of grace, of cultural engagement rather than subversion, are all gifts to be rediscovered and re-expressed in our Anglican tradition. Instead of looking towards either Rome or rationality, we need to encourage our ordinands and lay leadership to rediscover both the very nature and the depth of Anglican Evangelicalism.

Third, the *renewal* of communion. Anglican Evangelicalism represents a global catholicity that could empower wider Anglicanism into a truly worldwide Christian tradition. First, Evangelical unity across the Anglican Communion is a critical expression of catholicity. As Evangelical Christians we must never allow, either by the actions of others or by our own failings, catholicity to slip away. United in the truth of divine revelation, we have a head start. Second, we must express our Christian solidarity across global, national and racial boundaries, perhaps also across boundaries of style and emphasis. The crisis in the Communion has brought renewed opportunities for fellowship; we must work together, learn from one another, encourage each other, study together and demonstrate our unity as Anglican disciples of Jesus. Third, we must hold to account those who depart from our scriptural foundations and hence threaten to destroy, not just the Anglican Communion, but both Christian truth and Christian unity.

Fourth, *refocusing* upon mission and evangelism. This is not to suggest that other Christian or Anglican traditions are not committed to mission and evangelism, but rather to claim the unique opportunity for the Anglican Evangelical. The whole understanding of authority, purpose, doctrine, ministry and ecclesiology encourages Anglican Evangelicals to place mission and evangelism at the centre of their purposes and bring flexibility, creativity and passion to the task. This may indeed bring some challenges to the institutional Church in terms of parish boundaries, finance and the nature of ministerial leadership. However, a clarity to the message of the gospel and its life-saving power to transform is a central feature of Anglican Evangelicalism. The suggestion of tension with the institution is not an advocacy of free-for-all. Anglican Evangelicalism is well equipped to work creatively with this tension. However, as indicated in the challenges faced by the movement, the urgency of the claims of the gospel, together with institutional decline or even failure within Anglicanism, may increase the areas of tension and flashpoints. However, if the Anglican Evangelical tradition can bring to the wider Church creativity and urgency in areas of church growth and church planting, then it may be able to contribute to the renewal of the Anglican tradition rather than continued decline.

Fifth, *reasserting* the unity of Word and Spirit. Anglican Evangelicalism is well placed to ensure that both within the movement itself (with both its charismatic and Reformed strands) and within wider Anglicanism, Word and Spirit belong together and not apart. It is imperative for the future unity and vitality of the tradition that differing emphases on the nature and action of the Holy Spirit do not distract from the essential focus of gospel ministry. It is important to note that 'pentecostal' vitality has characterized the Evangelical movement from the beginning. Both historically and in the contemporary scene there have been those who have pushed the particular understanding of 'holiness', 'surrender', and 'intimacy' away from the foundations of Anglican Reformed doctrine. Yet, in moderate form, those same emphases have brought new life, a passion for Christ, for evangelism and for worship to the heart of Anglican Evangelicalism. Word and Spirit belong together. They are not to be separated by honest difference over the nature and practice of the supernatural gifts of the Spirit (speaking in tongues is no longer the mark that it was in the early days of Charismatic and Pentecostal renewal). It might also be that Anglican Evangelical unity of Word and Spirit can influence the wider tradition. The so-called Anglican *via media* was more a convenient invention of a modern form of Anglicanism that could not come to terms with the roots of the tradition. If Anglican Evangelicals can demonstrate the fullness of both Word and Spirit, just as they can illustrate the fullness of Anglican and Evangelical, then we might see the emergence of a much healthier Anglicanism: Church that does not need to continually assert equivalency of Scripture, reason and tradition or see itself as simply a middle way, but which might learn the benefit of both its own foundations and its subsequent development and expression, and not confuse the two.

It would be both inaccurate and inappropriate to claim the near or future prospect of the dominance of Evangelicalism within Anglicanism. There are many challenges from every angle. However, if Anglican Evangelicalism can become more confident in its own identity and purpose, and not be reduced to some sort of 'semi-Evangelical middle way' within Anglicanism, then there is the opportunity for significant advances for the gospel both for and within the Anglican tradition. The Church of England will, without doubt, be more Evangelical over the next phase of its existence. Evangelicals must bring to the table conviction, clarity, creativity, compassion and commitment within Anglicanism.

Notes

1   J. H. Pratt (ed.), (1865), *The Thought of the Evangelical Leaders: notes of the discussions of The Eclectic Society, London during the years 1798–1814*, reprinted 1978, Edinburgh, Banner of Truth, p. 224.

2   Ibid., p. 507.

3   D. L. Edwards and J. R. W. Stott (1988), *Essentials*, London, Hodder and Stoughton, p. 165.

4   P. F. M. Zahl (1998), *The Protestant Face of Anglicanism*, Grand Rapids, Eerdmans, pp. 59–69.

5   J. Wolffe (1991), *The Protestant Crusade in Great Britain 1829–1860*, Oxford, Clarendon Press.

6   One hundred and fifty members of the General Synod supported an amendment from the Bishop of Woolwich, the Rt Revd Colin Buchanan, when the Synod debated the report 'The Gift of Authority', on the matter of papal authority and the Marian decrees. *Report of Proceedings* (2004), General Synod, February Group of Sessions, vol. 35, no. 1, pp. 450–2, 464–7.

7   R. D. Turnbull (1993), 'The emergence of the Protestant Evangelical tradition', *Churchman*, vol. 107, no. 4.

8   P. Avis (1988), 'What is "Anglicanism"?' in S. Sykes & J. Booty (eds), *The Study of Anglicanism*, London, SPCK, p. 422.

9   T. E. Yates (1988), 'Anglicans and Mission', in Sykes and Booty, op. cit., pp. 429–41.

10 Rt Revd Katharine Jefferts Schori, Presiding Bishop-elect, homily preached at ECUSA General Convention, 21 June 2006, Episcopal News Service.

11 *Eucharistic Presidency: a theological statement by the House of Bishops of the General Synod* (1997), London, Church House Publishing, p. 41.

12 Ibid.

13 Ibid., p. 42.

14 *Bishop of Winchester's report* and *Archbishop's determination* in the matter of Canon c12(5) of the Canons of the Church of England between: The Revd Richard John Coekin, appellant and the Bishop of Southwark, respondent, Monday, 5 June 2006.

15 R. Jackson (2005), *The Road to Growth*, London, Church House Publishing and R. Jackson (2002), *Hope for the Church*, London, Church House Publishing, are both excellent contemporary reviews.

4

Church, culture and society

The claims of the gospel on society

Anglicanism in its various expressions and forms has always embodied the claims of the Christian gospel upon the transformation of society. Hence there is here potential for intra-Anglican conversation. The way in which the Christian gospel impacts upon society has been expressed differently in the several traditions and identities of Anglicanism. This has been true both theologically and pragmatically. To assess both the *common* and the *competing* claims of the Anglican and Evangelical upon society, as an objective of the transforming power of the gospel, we need to understand the different foundations from which the various traditions draw. It is inaccurate to characterize Evangelicalism more broadly, or Anglican Evangelicalism more particularly, as ignoring the social claims of the gospel. There are both common and competing claims. This can be seen in the theological origins of the social call of the gospel. The more Catholic and liberal strands within the Anglican tradition place the theological foundations for the social claims of the gospel within the doctrines of the *incarnation* and of *the Kingdom of God.* Evangelical Anglicans, in contrast, found their claims upon the *atonement.* Charismatic Evangelicals have also given weight to the theology of the kingdom (as a present and supernatural reality). On occasion this may have masked the dependency upon the atonement. The point here, though, is to note the original theological sources of differing approaches to social order. These distinctions are of crucial importance in understanding the differing emphases and for later appreciating the Evangelical basis for social concern.

The Catholic Anglican stress upon the incarnation has been the characteristic theological claim of that tradition. The identification of Christ with humanity as a consequence of the incarnation invests the whole of humanity with particular characteristics of the image of God. In addition, the taking by Jesus of human flesh identifies him with the claims of the body as well as of the soul. Hence this strand of the Anglican tradition has been long associated with social work across social and political boundaries and an especial identification with the poor. It was exemplified in the course of the nineteenth century by the work of the so-called 'ritual slum priests'. These were colourful characters (often in conflict with ecclesiastical authority) who combined a Catholic theology with a missionary zeal and a passionate concern for the welfare of the poor. This outlook, and its theological foundations, can be illustrated by Robert Dolling, the famous Anglo-Catholic priest of the Portsmouth slums: 'I speak out and fight about the drains because I believe in the incarnation.'[1] The same emphasis would be adopted within the more liberal strand of the Anglican tradition, but extended into the concept of the kingdom of God.

In the late 1870s and 1880s it was the great proponents of the liberal Anglican tradition, Brooke Foss Westcott, Charles Gore and Henry Scott Holland, not to mention William Temple in the 1920s, who appealed to Frederick Denison Maurice as the great progenitor of their thought. Maurice had developed an antipathy to theological and political systems, especially utilitarianism, the principle advocated by Jeremy Bentham of the objective of the greatest happiness of the greatest number. Maurice attacked competition, which he described as 'the selfish principle', and also the established notion, not least among theologians, that this 'destructive principle is a divine law'. Competition had negative impact upon the lives and conditions of the working classes. He advocated cooperative associations so that the benefits of capital could be gained for the workers although he was far from a socialist in economic understanding, despite the attack on competition. From this network of cooperatives, Maurice envisaged class harmony. He was not a political radical; he opposed trade unions and desired social harmony, believing that the way to achieve this was through the Christianization of the cooperative movement.

In 1838 Maurice published *The Kingdom of Christ*. He advocated the universal brotherhood of man under the eternal Fatherhood of God – central to the vision was the unity of Church and state. However, this union required the recognition of the true religious foundation of the social order of the state. The Kingdom of Christ, according to Maurice, was not to be reserved for some ethereal existence but was to be recognized in the social arrangements of humanity. God was immanent in the world in that his way and his will were made known within the self-consciousness of people. Christ is in every man. The kingdom is a present reality. The socialism in Maurice was not economic or political; rather it derived from his idea that all humanity constituted the living material of the spiritual and universal kingdom and that social behaviour which recognized Christ in another human was a form of reference to God himself. For Maurice his Christian socialism was primarily educative and ethical. He resisted political programmes and church parties, including at the end of the *Kingdom of Christ* an exhortation not to form a party to oppose all parties! The family and the nation were basic building blocks of the universal spiritual society. In the 1840s, in the lectures *The Religions of the World*, Maurice suggested that adherents of other religions were sincerely seeking God. Maurice became Professor of Theology at King's College, London in 1846. In 1853 he published his *Theological Essays*; in his essay 'Of eternal life and eternal death', Maurice rejected as superstitious the popular belief in the eternal punishment of the wicked and claimed such belief was not required by the Articles. The Council of King's deemed Maurice's doctrines to be dangerous and he was forced out from his chair.

Briefly, there are three ways in which this heritage has been set out in expressing the social claims of the gospel upon society. First, the Christian socialist movement. In the latter part of the nineteenth century this was promoted through a series of organizations drawing upon both the Catholic incarnational theology already referred to, together with the intellectual currents of Maurice and his successors. These societies were:

- The Guild of St Matthew
- The Christian Social Union
- The Church Socialist League

They were marked by incoherent leadership, intellectual remoteness and disagreement over politics and economics!

Stewart Headlam, founder of the Guild of St Matthew while curate of Bethnal Green in 1877, was deeply influenced by

Maurice. The objective was 'to promote the study of social and political questions in the light of the incarnation'. This was socialism covered with Catholic sacramentalism and Headlam soon found himself outside the boundaries of the Church. From 1878 to 1898 he was denied a licence by the Bishop. He stood bail for Oscar Wilde in 1895 when Wilde was put on charges for sodomy. Members resigned from the Guild: one commented that he was all for building the new Jerusalem but not for wading through Gomorrah first.

Rather different was the Christian Social Union founded in 1889. The key players were Henry Scott Holland, Charles Gore and Brooke Foss Westcott. This was respectable intellectual socialism – the recruits were from academia and the church hierarchy with no real contact with the emerging labour and trade union movement.

The Church Socialist League was founded in 1906 due to the 'indefiniteness' of the respectable CSU. No such vagueness for the League – socialism was embraced in economic as well as political terms. Yet there remained dissent over affiliation to the Independent Labour Party and there remained also a strong Anglo-Catholic link, not least to the Community of the Resurrection through Charles Gore and J. N. Figgis. Was the socialism to be espoused Catholic or secular? The tension was not resolved. The League split on several occasions. What was Christian socialism? It was a nice term, but an incoherent notion.

The origins of the social gospel movement on both sides of the Atlantic go back to these nineteenth- and early twentieth-century antecedents. The claims of the movement contrasted sharply with the Evangelical retreat from the world. The alignment of Christianity, especially Protestant Christianity, with the intellectual currents and forces of the time, led to increasing stress being laid upon the social claims of the gospel. Both in the USA and in England the gospel was seen increasingly in political terms; yet bizarrely many of the emphases were similar to the earlier Evangelical movement. However, as we shall see later in this chapter, the theological motivations were very different. In 1917 Walter Rauschenbusch wrote A Theology for the Social Gospel and he became an influential theologian of the movement. In England some of these themes were picked up by William Temple, Archbishop of Canterbury, 1942–1944. Temple had long involvement

in the social claims of the gospel under the influence of Maurice
and had been involved in the Workers' Educational Association,
the Labour Party and the World Council of Churches. He was also
influenced by the writings of R. H. Tawney and so his views developed in a particular corporatist and state-centred direction: one
of the classic presuppositions of much modern Anglican social
thought, to which we shall return.

Finally, to bring us further into the twentieth century. This
strand of the tradition was carried forward, first, by Bishop John
Robinson who challenged conventional orthodox theology with
his book *Honest to God*. Robinson, as Bishop of Woolwich, readily
adapted the gospel to the social circumstances of humanity. The
approach was essentially reductionist. The gospel was shorn of its
supernatural framework, values were reduced to 'love' and the
controlling theology was 'situation ethics'. Robinson was not
alone, for these were radical times. There was, however, also criticism of the secularization of the gospel.[2] The story could continue
with Bishop David Shepherd (from clearly Evangelical stock), the
impact of liberation theology, radical Evangelicals and the report
Faith in the City in 1985.

Anglican approaches to society and social welfare

Two case studies follow; one dealing with Anglican approaches to
education and the other with Anglican social theology, as exemplified in William Temple, but with its latest modern expression in
the report *Faithful Cities*.

Case study 1: Anglicans and education

Anglicanism has a long-standing commitment to and participation
in education at every level which continues right up to the present.
Currently some 25.2 per cent of all state primary schools are linked
in some way to the Church of England. Since many of these schools
are rural, the actual percentage of primary pupils attending Church
of England primary schools is somewhat smaller at 18.6 per cent.
These figures are significant. At the secondary level, the percentage
of schools and pupils is 5.8 per cent. There are three types of church
school. In a voluntary-aided school, the school is owned by the
governors, a majority of whom are appointed by the Church. The

governors are the employers and the admissions authority; there is usually distinctively Anglican religious education and worship and the Church contributes 10 per cent of the cost of repairs and capital. In voluntary-controlled schools (where in fact the control is less than in an aided school) the school is owned by the Church which appoints governors, but there is no church majority and the Local Education Authority (LEA) employs the teachers. The LEA funds capital and repairs, religious education follows the local agreed syllabus and the worship is Anglican. A foundation school is similar to a voluntary-controlled school except that the school is the employer and admissions authority. In 2001 the Church of England commissioned and published the report *The Way Ahead* under Lord Dearing, as part of its continuing work in and commitment to education. The Church embarked on an ambitious programme of expanding its involvement in the secondary sector by seeking an additional 100 church secondary schools; some 76 were at various stages of planning at October 2004, some 25 new schools having been opened or expanded.[3] What is the background to this involvement, how does it relate to Evangelical work in the same area and what are the issues raised?

The history of educational provision, not least for the poor, is long and complex. Nevertheless there was a period of considerable development and change in the period from around 1800–1870, the latter date marking the enactment of Forster's Education Act: compulsory state education. Given the nature of the Victorian period, it is not surprising that schools form part of the story for both Anglican and Evangelical Christians. It is worth noting at this point the development and spread of Sunday schools. Key names in this movement were Robert Raikes (1735–1811) and Hannah Moore (1745–1833). Raikes opened the first school in Gloucester in 1780; Moore developed schools around Cheddar, the first opening in 1789 involving religious instruction on Sundays and other activities for adults (especially mothers) on weekday evenings, such as knitting and sewing. Moral and spiritual improvement were key values. By 1815 there were two major societies promoting schools: the National Society and the British and Foreign School Society. The former adhered to the established Church, while the latter, founded in 1814, emphasized Bible reading and excluded denominational teaching. The number of children in schools doubled between

1820 and 1834, but both these groups faced considerable difficulty in achieving national coverage, providing buildings and
training teachers. The most common form of educational provision was a monitorial system whereby the older children taught
the younger. It was pioneered by Andrew Bell, an Anglican cleric,
who was prominent in the work of the National Society. On 16
October 1811 – the year of the death of Robert Raikes – the
'National Society for Promoting the Education of the Poor in the
Principles of the Established Church' (now known as the
National Society) was founded by, among others, Joshua Watson.
The stated aim was this: 'That the National Religion should be
made the foundation of National Education, and should be the
first and chief thing taught to the poor, according to the excellent
Liturgy and Catechism provided by our Church.'[4] The Society's
aim was to provide a church school in every parish. Grants were
offered and teachers were trained and the Society was also keen
to provide religious books for the students. Watson was closely
associated with a group of High Churchmen (the Hackney
Phalanx) and was over time involved with a variety of related
bodies, including the Additional Curates Society (founded in
response to the Church Pastoral Aid Society's insistence on the
principle of lay agency). There was a particular concern for the
privileges and duties of the established Church. Religious education and discipline and moral guidance featured amongst the
Society's subsidiary objectives. The key areas of difference
between this enterprise and that of the Evangelicals with their
Ragged Schools were these:

- The Ragged Schools aimed at the *poorest* in society; those
  excluded even from the National Schools
- The Evangelical school movement had a prior commitment to
  the Christian faith before the particulars of church government
  of the established Church
- The Ragged Schools had a passion for the Bible above more
  general religious instruction

The Ragged Schools, like the national schools, taught basic
educational disciplines and some handicraft-type skills; they also
suffered from many of the same problems. However, in taking this
analysis and seeking to apply it to the conversation between

Anglican and Evangelical today, the issues resonate with those of the past:

• How is the distinctively Christian ethos of the church school to be articulated and maintained?
• To what degree should church schools be independent of the state?
• What is the place of compulsory worship in schools?
• What is the nature of the commitment to the established Church?
• What does it mean to be Anglican?

The Evangelical challenge will be that of maintaining distinctiveness and a degree of independence from the state. They will be less concerned about promoting Anglicanism in either worship or ethos. The latter questions are, of course, issues that have run throughout this book; the modern presumption of a 'middle' or 'moderate Catholic' eucharistic-based Anglicanism sits no more at ease in the church schools sector than it does historically for Anglicanism as a whole. However, the contribution of the wider Anglican tradition is to bring this educational provision into the heart of both national and parochial life and vision. To that vision we will return at the conclusion of this chapter.

Case study 2: Anglican social theology from William Temple to Faithful Cities

William Temple probably stands as one of the twentieth century's leading figures in a number of ways, but not least for his understanding and exposition of social ethics. In doing so we can see the key features of the modern middle Anglican approach to these questions. Temple can be idolized and many of his observations have been uncritically adopted. By looking then at the recent *Faithful Cities* report[5] we can gain a picture into Anglican social ethics today and how Evangelicals can both relate to the tradition and critique it. Temple's *Christianity and Social Order* published in 1942 was a succinct summary of his social ethics. Temple rejected absolutes of moral conduct, whether constructed from the Bible or elsewhere.[6] That understanding of authority will immediately sound a warning note for Evangelicals. To Temple, circumstances are relevant to moral choice, there is no system that can be directly derived from Christianity and there is an 'irreducible element of uncertainty in moral choices', a fact to be relished rather than regretted.[7] Temple argues for two principles: that there is a difference between right and wrong, and that we have an obligation to do what is right. Temple is not denying all absolutes – the absolute is one of conscience, hence his concern for character. The injunction 'love thy neighbour as thy self' 'is the supreme principle of morality, the only absolute moral law'.[8] Temple develops his thought in terms of the sanctity of persons, the balancing of individual and community needs, of duties as much as of rights and of responsible citizenship.

So at the heart of Temple's *Christianity and Social Order* lies his exposition of primary and secondary principles. The primary principles are God and his purposes, and man, his dignity, tragedy and destiny. The secondary principles are freedom, social fellowship and service. Towards the end of the book Temple asserts the priority of natural law and the key Christian principles of love and justice. Temple works with a dialectic method with these principles and in his appendix sets out his 'programme for action', in the context of his times. He was developing the middle axiom: the middle way between principles and policy prescription. Such an approach has continued to inform modern Anglican social ethics. Evangelicals would always be cautious of treating the biblical revelation in any secondary way or by divesting it of its ultimate authority. That, of course, is not incompatible with either developing principles or middle axioms. One of the tensions in Temple's thought is that philosophically he seems to be rejecting absolute biblical principles, yet in practice he can seem to be deriving such principles exactly from the biblical revelation.

A useful insight into where modern Anglican social theology has positioned itself can be gained from the report *Faithful Cities* published in May 2006 by an ecumenical Commission on Urban Life and Faith. The very title of the report conveys the ambiguity which would generate questions from Evangelicals. How can 'cities' be 'faithful'? The foreword to the work gives weight to *experience* and *empiricism* before *theology* and the theology articulated is the classic emphasis on kingdom and incarnation. Hence the approach is essentially inductive. Thus Baroness Richardson, the Chair of the Commission, gives prominence to the people met, the stories heard and the deepening of understanding on issues such as injustice. The last sentence of the introduction reads: 'Beyond all this is the conviction that God is in the city and the kingdom of God is at hand.'[9] The report notes that things have changed since *Faith in the City*. These include the context of a multi-faith society, work patterns, urban regeneration but also new concepts of partnership between state and voluntary sector. This last point is noted in contrast to the presumed alternatives of state initiative or private voluntary sector of two decades earlier.[10] In turning to the theological concepts that are the building blocks, incarnation and resurrection are mentioned (but not atonement) and God's faithfulness. Incarnation (God's being alongside his people) and faithfulness are linked by the concept of sustainability – and this is summarized in the idea of 'faithful capital'. This concept is linked to the idea of social capital (the value of social relationships and participation) but made distinctive by the fact it resides in 'faith communities', the spirituality of faith communities and congregations, 'historically expressed in the major world faiths'.[11] The report describes the common core values:

- God as the source of life
- Humanity made in the image of God, giving dignity
- Humanity in relationship with God with values of mutuality, love and justice

Thus emphasis is given to relationships modelling the divine relationships, the sacredness of life and the idea of human flourishing in the common life. The social and political idea of regeneration is given faithful currency when it is combined with the language of love, hope, judgement, forgiveness, remembrance and hospitality. The report sets out a range of other emphases:

- Importance of the presence of faith communities in urban areas
- Hospitality across boundaries of race and creed replacing fear
- Partnership with the agents and agencies of regeneration
- The increasing gap between poor and prosperous
- Empowerment and participation

The major dividend of faithful capital is people motivated by a moral sense that other people and their circumstances matter. There is a duty and purpose-driven enthusiasm for regeneration and transformation – and not simply in some mystical or spiritualized sense. Often this bears fruit in partnerships across what would commonly be regarded as divides . . .[12]

In Chapter 7, the report asks why faith communities are involved in partnerships concerned with urban regeneration. The key points which are drawn out are these:

- The biblical concept of transformation, seen as essentially communal
- The biblical theme of perfection, seen in the city of the New Jerusalem
- The experience of the exodus and the wandering in the desert
- Covenant
- Jubilee
- The Christian commitment to justice exemplified by Jesus at the Last Supper

In summary:

We have the ongoing task of translating the will of this transcendent God into the realities of day-to-day politics. We are therefore called to analyse, understand and critique the structures, policies and programmes we encounter. Our struggle for God's reign involves acting as advocates for those whose voice is rarely heard, and empowering the excluded. We are compelled to stand alongside them and to form alliances with them and with others who work for the same purposes.[13]

The report gives weight to the core values that are shared across the religious divides, including peace and cooperation, social justice and equity and the loving of neighbour. The government approach, partially due to the gap in social provision, is to form partnerships with faith communities. These are expressed at a number of levels including that of Local Strategic Partnerships bringing together in one forum all of those concerned with regeneration in a locality. Nevertheless, it is worth noting that many

Evangelical churches still struggle to achieve any funding partnerships with local authorities due to both the *distinctiveness* of the
Church and *control* by the Church. Many powerful examples were
drawn of church and community involvement, the provision of
community facilities, relationships with health centres, the arts,
education and enterprise. Perhaps in the years since *Faith in the
City* the place of entrepreneurial enterprise has been seen in
more positive light as part of this complex web of social relationships that contribute towards regeneration. How is all of this to be
evaluated and assessed? We will return at the end of this chapter
to an articulation of how Anglican and Evangelical exponents of
social reform can better understand each other, and what are the
opportunities and the tensions. The *Faithful Cities* report,
however, stands as a current model of how 'middle' Anglicanism
approaches social questions. In summary this can be seen as:

• Incarnational theology
• Partnerships across divides are essential without compromising
  Christian distinctives
• The Church's ministers are not, generally, called to be full-time
  social entrepreneurs
• Partnerships must include those with private enterprise
• There is an obligation to highlight the plight of the poor

There are many synergies with the heritage of Anglican social
theology and links into the theology and practice of Christian socialism and its history. There are some areas where Anglican Evangelicals would wish to qualify or add or subtract. This would include the
questions of inter-faith cooperation, Christian distinctiveness,
atonement theology, the socio-economic policy presumptions and
holding social welfare and evangelism together in the Church's
theology of mission. However, two other points need to be made.
First, the shift in emphasis in the last two decades towards a recognition of the role of the (wide range) of Evangelical churches
involved in social action and social reform. Second, the change that
has taken place over that time to draw a broader economic view of
potential partners. For the Evangelical there is here a good deal
which can be identified with, worked with and developed in partnership for the glorious good of our cities and urban environments,
and for the sake of the gospel. More of that later.

The Evangelical heritage of social reform

Evangelicalism has a glorious heritage of social welfare and reform that was combined with the commitment to evangelism and produced significant fruit and impact in society. This part of the history of Evangelicalism has been often ignored but perhaps in recent years has experienced something of a resurgence of interest. There is still a great deal to learn about the theological background and undergirding of the period in the nineteenth century (1835–1870 perhaps representing the high point) when Evangelicalism was at its most potent in the transformation of industrial England. The reasons for the decline of this emphasis within the Evangelical tradition are also instructive. It has been remarked that 'as many as three-quarters of the total number of voluntary charitable organizations in the second half of the nine-teenth century can be regarded as Evangelical in character and control',[14] and the Earl of Shaftesbury commented in 1884, shortly before his death, that 'most of the great philanthropic movements of the century have sprung from the Evangelicals'.[15] The questions are how and why and what changed?

Impact of theological change within Evangelicalism

Some key events were taking place in the 1820s. First, CMS was expanding and so much so that it seemed at least to its patrons that CMS would soon take the world for the gospel, and not just for the gospel, but also for the British Empire, the Church of England and the Book of Common Prayer. CMS was leading the Church, it was thought, into a glorious future. Indeed the future into which the Church was being led was nothing less than the millennium of Revelation 20 (see Chapter 2). Slowly but surely the prosperity which CMS was bringing in the gospel would lead into this period of glorious blessedness. Second, however, all was not well at home. In industrial England the movement of popula-tion from the countryside into the town led to increasing squalor in London and other cities. Where was the gospel for the working man or woman? Indeed, what did the gospel have to say to the condition of industrial England? No millennium here. Third, this pessimism also infected the Churches with increasing criticism of what was seen as reliance on human means (as exemplified by

CMS) rather than divine means, and emphasis on sin, judgement and the negative 'signs of the times'.

These trends played out in three ways. First, the theological change, referred to in Chapter 2, as Evangelicals came increasingly to embrace a premillennial understanding of the Second Advent rather than the postmillennialism of CMS. This reflected a pessimistic view of society, which would require the sudden intervention of God with the return of Christ to usher in the new age, which would return the Churches to purity and society's evils would be corrected. The premillennial understanding of the Second Advent was to be a significant element in Evangelical social reform. Second, on the ground, the premillennial advent was accompanied by outbreaks of *glossolalia*, speaking in tongues, in Cambuslang near Glasgow, and in the London church of the prominent premillennialist, The Revd Edward Irving. The great and the good rolled up in their carriages to Irving's church to witness the events and his own dramatic coming under the power of the Spirit. Third, a hardening of the Protestantism of Evangelical theology. If the Lord was soon to return he would expect to find purity in his Church. So, the Apocrypha crisis in the Bible Society in 1825–27; in 1827 the founding of the Protestant Reformation Society; in 1828 the establishment of a newspaper, *The Record*. The Protestant crusade was under way.[16] There were at least 30 Members of Parliament, all Tories, known as *Recordites* because of their association with the Evangelicalism of *The Record*, including the son of a former assassinated prime minister, Spencer Percival M.P., Michael Sadler M.P. and Sir Robert Inglis, the M.P. for the University of Oxford. These figures were prominent also in the fight for social reform. Wilberforce, just a few years before his death, voted for Catholic emancipation – in the eyes of most Evangelicals an act of apostasy. With the onward march of historicist premillennialism, the papacy and Rome were increasingly associated with the beast, the whore of Babylon and other apocalyptic figures.

The future leader of Anglican Evangelicalism, Anthony Ashley Cooper (Lord Ashley), later the 7th Earl of Shaftesbury, entered Parliament in 1825. He was converted to Christ in the following couple of years, made his first parliamentary speech on the subject of the treatment of mental health patients, supported Catholic emancipation (and then regretted it), and by the mid-1830s was a convinced premillennialist. All his envelopes carried labels declaring 'come Lord Jesus', and he was a close friend of Edward Bickersteth, another premillennialist, who later became secretary of CMS. The impact upon social reform of the change in theological perception in respect of the millennium will be discussed further later in this chapter.

Evangelical voluntary societies

The setting for much Evangelical activity was the parish. The basic parish system of the Church of England remained corrupt in many ways, but most especially so up to 1836. There was widespread non-residence, pluralism and simony. The worst examples were the vicarage of Stanhope in County Durham (which carried with it an extraordinary annual stipend of £18,000) and the Golden Stalls of Durham Cathedral (£3,000). In 1831 the Bishop of Durham had an income of £22,000 per annum. It was, at this stage, the Evangelicals who stepped into the parochial ministry to serve the people of God under their care. So long excluded, but with footholds gained through lectureships and proprietary chapels, now they led the way as they sought to minister to the masses of industrial Victorian England. New societies emerged. The early Evangelicals had established the less than successful London Missionary Society in 1795 – the first inter-denominational society. Anglican Evangelicals founded the CMS in 1799 and in 1804 the Bible Society was established; the first genuinely successful inter-denominational society gathered around the single goal of Bible distribution. As has been illustrated previously, this did not exempt the Society from the impact of the quest for purity in the 1820s. CPAS, under Lord Ashley's watchful eye, was founded in 1836, just one year after the inter-denominational London City Mission (LCM). Evangelicals now began more explicitly to cooperate across denominational lines, Ashley again at the helm. CPAS was founded on the principle of 'the gospel to every door with a single eye to the glory of God'. The Society advocated lay workers in industrial parishes. The balloon went up. Some early high Church supporters including Gladstone left, and Bishop Blomfield of London sought to oppose and oppress the Society; he later became a convinced supporter! Lord Shaftesbury was England's most prominent Evangelical in the middle of the nineteenth century. He founded or was closely associated with numerous great societies, including:

- The Church Pastoral Aid Society
- The London City Mission
- The Ragged School Union
- The London Society for the Promotion of Christianity Among the Jews
- The Colonial and Continental Church Society
- The British and Foreign Bible Society
- The Church Missionary Society

We see, simply in this list, the combination of the Evangelistic zeal and a passion for social reform. It was a powerful combination. One consequence of Evangelicals beginning to work the parishes of Victorian England was that they met the poverty of Victorian England. Lord Shaftesbury led the Evangelical cause for social reform based upon gospel principles, together with personal experience, not least walking the streets of London in the company of the City missionaries. Shaftesbury was responsible for legislation on mental health, factories, hours of labour, housing, chimney sweeps and sanitation, to name but a few. Through these societies he worked with, he supported schools, making provision for poor workers such as flower girls and barrow boys, and at all times the gospel and social reform (eternal need and temporal need) were combined. His motivation was essentially the atonement (Christ died for these poor chimney sweeps) and the Second Coming (discipleship in preparation for the Lord's return).

By way of illustration there is Shaftesbury's relationship with the LCM. He was, of course, a passionate advocate of the LCM's principles of Evangelical catholicity and lay agency. Shaftesbury himself never had an official position within the LCM but was a regular speaker at its annual meetings. His links were much more with the individual missionaries, such as Thomas Jackson, the 'missionary to the thieves'. Shaftesbury was in no doubt at all that the LCM was committed to the temporal as well as the eternal welfare of the citizens of London, reflecting his own theological concern with the unity of body and soul, together with his eschatological understanding. Shaftesbury unashamedly stated that the LCM's operations had social as well as religious and even political aspects. The City missionary penetrated the darkest alleys and places of the metropolis; the society was, according to Shaftesbury, in a unique position to watch for, and counteract, the rise and progress of evil, be it physical or spiritual. A significant amount of the evidence gathered by Shaftesbury for use in his campaigns for social reform was gathered in cooperation with the missionaries of the LCM. One of these social reforms was the reform of the common lodging house. These houses provided accommodation, mainly communal, for poor workers and others who could not afford any other accommodation; they were controlled by private landlords and the conditions were marked by filth and squalor. At the opening of the LCM's new headquarters in 1874, Shaftesbury noted that the first intimation of the scandal of the lodging houses had been given to him by a City missionary and that the evidence he had presented to the House of Commons 'came entirely from the labours of the London City Mission'. He told the 1848 annual meeting: 'I ought to stand forward at this emergency, and declare what I have seen and heard in my many peregrinations through the dens and recesses of this metropolis in company with your admirable and devoted missionaries.'[17] In an introduction to a book about the City Mission, Shaftesbury added: 'In all difficulties of research, our first resource was to the City missionaries, because we knew that their enquiry would be zealous and immediate, and their report ample and trustworthy.'[18]

The two names that feature most regularly in Shaftesbury's connections with the LCM were Thomas Jackson and Roger Miller. He met over the course of three meetings with thieves in Jackson's company in 1848 a total of 394 felons. Jackson was clearly concerned, like Shaftesbury, with both social and spiritual well-being. Shaftesbury frequently visited Jackson and his work, sometimes even unannounced. Roger Miller died in a railway accident in 1848. Shaftesbury noted that he had been a close and intimate friend and that day and night they had walked the streets of London, making use of the information gained in his speeches in the House of Commons. They had both been closely involved in the Broadwall Ragged School where Miller had gathered 130 children into the school, closely supported by Shaftesbury. After Miller's death, Shaftesbury appealed for financial help for his family through a letter in *The Times*. Shaftesbury's work with the Ragged Schools kept him close to the City missionaries. The

Ragged School movement had originated with the LCM before becoming independent, after the Mission chose not to adopt the work officially. In 1848 at the annual meeting of the LCM, Shaftesbury recalled the link saying: '. . . whenever you enter a Ragged School, remember this – we are indebted for nine-tenths of them to the humble, the pious, the earnest City missionary'.[19]

The Ragged Schools had a very significant impact upon the education of the poor in London. They were independent schools, established by benefactors, designed to provide basic education and scriptural teaching to the poor, the 'ragged' often excluded from whatever other schooling provision was available, excluded by poverty, clothing and class. Teams of volunteers, many of them women, organized and ran the Ragged Schools which, from 1844 onwards, were gathered together into the Ragged School Union under Lord Shaftesbury's guidance. We must not over-romanticize the movement. The schools were concerned with Bible teaching and religious services, moral welfare and also social provision of clothing, and later also with lodging and, certainly at Christmas, with meals.

Legislative action

One of the great strengths of the Evangelical movement in the nineteenth century was that it combined legislative action with voluntary societies. It did not rely, in respect of its social reforming work, only on one and not the other. The enormous advantage was that the movement was able to maintain its Christian distinctiveness, retain its emphasis on evangelism and yet also demonstrate a holistic understanding of the human condition and be seen to take action for its change and improvement. Shaftesbury is the example, *par excellence*, of parliamentary reforming work from a Christian basis and understanding. Shaftesbury made hundreds of speeches to Parliament, both in the House of Commons and later in the House of Lords – some 243 speeches between 1836–1884. He sponsored legislation, promoted Bills and reforms and at all times invested his work with his Evangelical Christian faith. His parliamentary work covered these areas:

- Factory reform
- Industrial reform and employment

- Public health
- Lunacy reform
- Foreign affairs
- Protestantism
- Other ecclesiastical issues
- Education

Mental health, factory reform and climbing boys can be used for illustration. Those who care for and seek to provide for the sick in mind rarely receive public accolade. Potentially, though, Shaftesbury's work in connection with the afflicted in mind – to which he devoted himself longer than any other cause – could rank as his noblest achievement. In February 1828 mental health was the subject of his first major speech to Parliament. From 1829 Shaftesbury acted as the Chairman of the Metropolitan Lunacy Commission, extended in 1845 to cover the whole nation with Shaftesbury as its permanent Chairman. He remained so until his death. By the 1830s many counties had built asylums to house the most seriously afflicted of the mentally ill; however, there was no provision for the inspection and monitoring of the asylums and the conditions for the poor patients were wretched. The job of the lunacy commissioners was to visit, inspect and license; visiting without notice, day and night. Shaftesbury was a most active commissioner and many of the scenes he witnessed were harrowing, but through his determination and hard work he gradually brought about an improvement in conditions. It was Shaftesbury who introduced the 1845 legislation to establish a permanent Lunacy Commission in his speech using the evidence he had gathered as a commissioner visiting the asylums.

Second, factory reform. The industrialization of England led to significantly increased competition and desire for profit among manufacturers, hence shift working was introduced and the demand for child labour increased. By an Act of 1831 children under the age of 18 were not permitted to work more than 12 hours per day. The report of the Evangelical Tory M.P., Michael Sadler, in 1832 had exposed horrific working conditions. From this emerged the Ten Hours Movement, a strange coalition of Tory paternalists, Evangelicals (these first two categories often combined) and working-class organizations such as the Short Time Committees. After Sadler lost his seat in Parliament it was

Shaftesbury who emerged as the Ten Hours champion. The Bill he introduced (restricting women and children under 18 to a maximum of ten hours' work per day) was ultimately amended by the government of the day. Thus, the Factory Act of 1833 (Mills and Factories Act) brought in a number of reforms and requirements and included a restriction on working hours for children under 13 to nine hours per day and 48 hours per week. The reduction from 18 years to 13 years as the threshold for lifting the restrictions was a late government amendment, opposed by Shaftesbury. Employers got round the system by way of 'relays'. Sets of children working within the time limits could support older children, women and adults working way in excess (and keeping the younger children within the factory environment). It was not until 1844 that working time restrictions for women and children under 18 finally prevailed, with a limit on both daily and weekly work in the factory. Further reform for adult males was yet to follow. Shaftesbury was also concerned with a wide range of industrial reform – consider his speech in 1840 for a commission into the employment of children in mines and factories:

. . . I have been bold enough to undertake this task, because I must regard the objects of it as being created, as ourselves, by the same Maker, redeemed by the same Saviour, and destined to the same Immortality . . .[20]

Another area of industrial concern was that of chimney sweeps. Sweeps employed children as young as five or six years old to climb the narrow flues to clean them. Some became stuck in the chimneys, many died from inhalation of fumes or the effects of toxic gases from the hearths and the fires. The legislation in force, the Chimney Sweeps Act of 1834, which banned the apprenticing of boys under ten years old, was ineffective due to lack of enforcement. Lord Ashley supported or introduced legislation to Parliament to ban the employment of children as sweeps in 1840, 1853–56, 1864 and in 1875 when the practice was finally outlawed through effective enforcement. He presented evidence of children being stolen and forced into the sweeps' employment; pins were stuck into their feet and lighted fires had been used to force the children up the chimneys. The children suffered sores, bruises and burns. He described the practice as satanic. The rich, he said, preferred not to ask how their chimneys were cleaned. The country could never claim to be Christian while such practices continued and the earlier laws continued to be broken.

Theological principles

What were the theological principles which underlay this powerful understanding and approach to evangelism and social reform? Shaftesbury and his views stand as illustrative and instructive. To Shaftesbury, mission was an essential part of his Evangelicalism. He saw the established Church of England and its parochial system as an effective and wise pattern for mission. Alongside this he advocated the radical reform of evening worship to cater for the needs of the working man and supported the holding of services in the open air and in theatres. The theological foundations of this approach revolved around the following aspects of Evangelical identity:

• The Bible and Protestantism
• Catholicity
• Lay agency
• Unity of body and soul
• Eschatology

The Bible and Protestantism

Shaftesbury's high view of Scripture meant that he gave a prominent place to the Bible in missionary work. The poor had as much a right of access to the Scriptures as the rich and wealthy, indeed it was that access to God's very word which gave protection from clerical domination. What the Scriptures taught, not least in terms of welfare, was to be obeyed and the injunctions were very strong indeed.

Catholicity

Evangelical catholicity, as we have seen elsewhere, was an essential weapon in the armoury of the Evangelical movement. It was this principle that was put into practice in many of the voluntary societies in respect of both evangelism and social welfare. Shaftesbury saw all the great societies in this light – this is what he said about the Bible Society:

One important view of the Society is, that it is catholic in character – catholic in all its operations; that it enables us to form in these realms, in times of singular distress and difficulty, a solemn league and covenant of all those who 'love the Lord Jesus Christ in sincerity', that it shows how, suppressing all minor differences, or treating them as secondary, members of the Church of England and Nonconformists may band together in one great effort, not only of resistance to, but, I hope, of aggression on, Popery and Satan.[21]

Yes, of course, in his usual Protestant fashion, popery and Satan are linked there, but the power of the quotation lies in its emphasis on Evangelical catholicity. Then this in respect of the LCM:

. . . put all that aside, and let all establishments and all distinctive Churches sink into the ground, compared with the one great effort to preach the doctrine of Christ crucified to every creature on the earth, to every creature that can be reached on this habitable globe.[22]

Shaftesbury was something of an enigma in pan-Evangelical cooperation. He remained devoted to the established Church as an Evangelical, yet was also critical of dissent whilst firmly committed to united action. He was an idealist, and cooperation across the Evangelical spectrum remained a significant feature and reality in his life and work.

Lay agency
This was another key aspect of pan-Evangelicalism. In Shaftesbury's view, lay agency was 'absolutely and essentially necessary', indeed, a principle never to be departed from. Shaftesbury himself said: 'I hold myself to be, and I hold all my brethren to be, lay-agents.'[23] Lay agency was of particular importance in the task of bringing the gospel to the changing industrial and urban scene of Victorian England. Both CPAS and the LCM were based upon the principle espoused by Shaftesbury that '. . . if you wish to win working men, you must enlist for that service a vast body of the working men themselves.'[24] The use of the lay agent was the only way that the gospel would penetrate into the depths of London,

into those areas denied to the ordained minister. This again all fits in with the vision for the Ragged Schools, staffed by volunteer lay teachers with that same ability to reach out. So Shaftesbury defended lay agency both as a theological principle and as a practical necessity.

Unity of body and soul

The theological unity of body and soul formed part of Shaftesbury's eschatological belief. This principle led logically to the Christian's having as much concern for the body, its physical, social, temporal and material welfare, as for the soul, the eternal, the spiritual, the final destination, the ultimate status before God. Shaftesbury always sought to hold these elements together in his understanding of mission. He viewed concern for body and soul as equally the work of the gospel. Earthly matters could not be separated from heavenly. It is, therefore, a common inaccuracy to consider the Evangelical movement as concerned only with the future of the soul.

Eschatology

Eschatology is the theology of the 'end times'. As has been seen, this aspect of theology was particularly prominent in the Evangelicalism of the nineteenth century. It had an especial importance in respect of responses to social welfare. The various views set out in Chapter 2 had implications for social reform and the holding together of evangelism and social welfare. The more extreme historicist premillennialist tended to be a quietist in the face of the imminent return of Christ – the calculation of the date for which was a compelling activity. If the Lord is to return soon, then surely there is nothing to do now, for all will be reversed. However, the moderate historicist premillennialist came to the point of urgency of action and Christian discipleship in the light of the imminence of the second advent. This was precisely because the signs indicated the time was 'near', though unknown; therefore we had responsibilities in the interim, and what would the Lord find us doing when he returned? The futurist or dispensationalist premillennialist saw the reversal of our current peril and condition as belonging to a future dispensation – not requiring any immediate action. The postmillennial view looked for a gradual improvement mainly in morals and suffered from an overly optimistic assessment of current circumstances. The amillennial view carries the disadvantage of lack of urgency.

Shaftesbury was a moderate historicist premillennialist. He believed in the imminency of the second coming, of the signs of the times and the gradual worsening of the human condition. He did not, however, seek to match year by year, decade by decade, features of the historicist approach to the chapters of the book of Revelation or seek to guess a date for the second advent. It was this sort of dynamic that helped him to avoid quietism and advocate and pursue both spiritual and social action. Neglect of our duty in the period before the second advent would lead to judgement. Our calling was to faithful discipleship:

> The time is coming when matters will not be measured by the talent, or the ability, or by fine clothes, or by power to speak, or by being on platforms, or by listening to those upon platforms; but the time is coming when matters will be measured by those who have the truest faith, the deepest love, and the most sincere acts of obedience to their Lord and Saviour, and most devoted and strong imitation of his blessed example.[25]

And finally:

> I am now looking, not to the great end, but to the interval. I know, my friends, how great and glorious that end will be; but while I find so many persons looking to no end, and others rejoicing in that great end, and thinking nothing about the interval, I confess that my own sympathies and fears dwell much with what must take place before that great consummation.[26]

Decline and revival

John Stott in *Issues Facing Christians Today*, a volume published in 1984 to contribute to the reforging of a contemporary response to social need and social issues amongst the Evangelical world, noted both the glorious heritage of Evangelical social concern and its decline. Assessing the reasons for this 'great reversal', Stott draws attention to the following:

- The priority of the fight against theological liberalism
- Reaction against 'the social gospel'
- Disillusion and pessimism following the First World War
- The impact of the spread of premillennialism
- The inhabitation of middle-class culture by Evangelicals

These reasons are clearly part of the picture but there is more to say. Stott specifies the spread of the premillennial scheme of J. N. Darby as the background to his comment. It is very important to realize that this view was that of futurist or dispensational premillennialism; it is particularly significant to recall that other forms of premillennialism were a major encouragement to Evangelical social reform.

There are two other factors to which attention needs to be drawn:

- The impact of government intervention in the voluntary sector
- Evangelical preoccupation with matters of internal dispute

The impact of the Forster Education Act of 1870 was deeply significant for Evangelical voluntary social action. It was a major intervention of the state into the traditional realm of Evangelical social concern. Education was now to be provided via local school boards. The number of Ragged Schools plummeted in the decade following 1870. This is not so much a comment upon the propriety of that particular Act of Parliament; more to note the impact it had on the Evangelical mindset. The state was now taking major steps into voluntary social provision; education was simply a key example. The consequence was the increased withdrawal of Evangelicals from that voluntary sector. One of the major planks and strengths of the Evangelical social witness had been its dynamic ability to combine governmental action and voluntary response. If the second of these were to be removed, then it was much harder for Evangelicals to distinguish their approach from that of the social gospel or political activists. The resultant withdrawal was catastrophic for Evangelical self-understanding.

This was reinforced by the excessive concern of Evangelicals for ecclesiastical politics. This failing, too, has continued. In the latter half of the nineteenth century, fuelled by the anti-Catholicism that has always featured within Evangelical identity, Evangelicals turned inwards. They battled, in church, in law and on the streets over ecclesiastical drapery and finery. Preservation of identity, resistance to creeping Catholicism within Anglicanism may indeed have been important contests. However, it caused Evangelicals to look away from society and into the Church, it absorbed enormous energy, inflicted pain and led to a loss of credibility. The jailing of Anglo-Catholic clergy under the Public Worship Regulation Act, promoted by Shaftesbury, merely confirmed the loss of confidence and sense of direction.

Modern resurgence

In 1967, amid growing confidence amongst Anglican Evangelicals, the first National Evangelical Anglican Congress included assertions of Evangelical social concern. In 1968 TEAR Fund (The Evangelical Alliance Relief Fund) was established (or re-established from a small existing fund) and grew into one of the most significant expressions of Evangelical social action over the subsequent four decades. There was also the emergence, first of the Nationwide Festival of Light in 1971, with a passion for the moral state of the nation, and then as a successor in 1983 of CARE – Christian Action, Research and Education. CARE continues to lobby government, educate and inform and campaign on a range of moral and social matters of concern to Evangelical Christians.

On the international level, gatherings of Evangelicals have also given more prominence to the social agenda. The Berlin Congress in 1966 saw social issues feature on its agenda, including a condemnation of racism, and the Wheaton Congress criticized Evangelical isolation from the world. These were first steps, but significant ones. Prominent personalities such as John Stott, Samuel Escobar and René Padilla were all slowly raising, or re-raising, the profile. Part of the international complexity was continuing tension between the social gospel agenda of the World Council of Churches and the international Evangelical movement. The International Congress on World Evangelization met in Lausanne, Switzerland, in July 1974 with half of the 2,500 participants from the developing world. Very early on, in addresses to the conference, Billy Graham and John Stott asserted the importance of both evangelism and social action. Escobar and Padilla were other prominent advocates. The outcome was the

Lausanne Covenant and also the Lausanne movement. The Covenant, even in its pre-conference draft, affirmed social action. However, in the light of the Conference discussions, the wording was strengthened, affirming 'not only social care or philanthropy but also social reform'.[27] The Lausanne commitments have been carried forward by the Lausanne Committee for World Evangelization.

There are many other features of the story, including a wide range of tensions, not least the association of Evangelical social concern with the political Left, which as well as damaging the cause in the USA has in England led to over-optimism concerning the role of government and an uncritical adoption of Keynesian economic policy presumptions. The reality of social policy is considerably more complex. On the international scale, HIV, poverty and debt relief now feature on Evangelical agendas. The same loose thinking often applies, and uncritical assertions of the priority of debt relief, for example, which fail to take into account that the most indebted countries are not synonymous with the poorest countries, discredit Evangelical social thought. It also shows the failure to appreciate the heritage of the movement and its careful balance of intervention and action at both government and voluntary level.

Recapturing the imagination of society?

Upon his appointment as Archbishop of Canterbury in July 2002, Rowan Williams talked about the need for the 'Christian faith to recapture the imagination of our people and our culture'. Less than six months later he was reinforcing some of these thoughts in the Richard Dimbleby Lecture. In assessing the place and role of the religious tradition in the nation state, Archbishop Williams affirmed the value and the place of religious communities in terms of opening up the depth of human choices and resources for human identity. So far from the religious community being relegated to the private sphere, its presence, partnership and engagement are vital. This means also defending the intellectual credibility of the faith.[28] In respect of the role of the Church in statutory education, the Archbishop went on to say:

To point to the importance of religious communities as, for example, partners in statutory education, is not to license unbridled superstition and indoctrination, but to invite – to challenge – religious communities to find a way of bringing their beliefs into practical contact with public questions, to identify exactly what difference faith commitments make to the educational process.[29]

And more generally:

In the pre-modern period, religion sanctioned the social order; in the modern period it was a potential rival to be pushed to the edges, a natural reaction. But we are at the point where, as the 'public sphere' becomes more value free, the very survival of the idea of a public sphere, a realm of political argument about vision and education, is going to demand that we take religion a good deal more seriously.[30]

These are important comments in the continuing development of social ethics, engagement and articulation of vision for Christians generally, for Anglican Christians and for Evangelicals within and without the Church of England. What are the prospects for agreement, particularly between the wider Anglican and Evangelical traditions concerning this social vision, and where are the tensions? The broad Anglican tradition brings with it a heritage of involvement and engagement with society, a passion for the development of a social ethic and a relationship with the wider society that opens up both opportunity and responsibility. There are three areas where Anglicans and Evangelicals (not least, of course, Anglican Evangelicals) can agree. In each case there is a challenge to the Evangelical, but also the Evangelical will wish to offer a modest qualification.

First, the new opportunities *for partnerships* between public and private sector are an important development. These partnerships are entirely consistent with the imagination which the Archbishop of Canterbury has sought to articulate in bringing the Christian ethic to bear upon wider society. This approach values both public and voluntary spheres, private enterprise as well as public intervention – the Evangelical will celebrate this approach alongside the broader Anglican tradition. The challenge to the Evangelical is to recognize two things: first, that this approach fits well with the classic Evangelical commitment to social reform; second, that this is a move and a development away from simply restating corporatist economic models which have perhaps dominated or been too much presumed in previous socio-economic discussion. The qualification which the Evangelical brings is also twofold: first, the Evangelical will wish to maintain a clear Christian distinctive in the approach, the debate and the engagement; second, the Evangelical will wish to maintain a place for the Evangelical voluntary society alongside other models of engagement. An example here might be in youth work provision. Evangelicals will wish to work in partnership with public authorities in the provision of youth work, not least in areas of particular need (which are not always deprived). However, many local authorities decline to give financial or other support to church youth work unless the faith perspective is denied and control removed to a secular management committee. For partnerships to be effective with faith communities, government needs to ensure that there are no such restrictions which fail to honour the meaning of partnership.

Second, the shared commitment of the Anglican and the Evangelical to *education*, not least to the education of the most disadvantaged children in society, is to be celebrated and welcomed. The commitment of the Church of England to the education system, to the historic responsibility towards universal education, and to a passion for the education of the disadvantaged, provides enormous opportunity for development. The Evangelical will welcome this heritage and this commitment since it is a shared one. The challenge that this brings to the Evangelical world is to resist the temptation to establish separate Christian schools which cream off Christian children into a protected environment and hence weaken the broader Evangelical witness. That is not to say that private education is wrong and it is not to say there is no place for private Christian education. It is also manifestly the case that the educational system in the USA is so significantly different from that in England, that a quite different approach would be warranted there. It is, however, to assert, at least in England, that Christian parents should consider first of all, and prior to any commitment to private education, how they can best support Christian involvement and witness in their local schools, in particular, but not exclusively, church schools. The challenge which the Evangelical brings to education again revolves around the importance of the Christian distinctive. This would include the ability to maintain an explicit Christian ethos, make appointments of those with Christian faith, admissions which recognize (albeit not exclusively) that faith and a breadth which goes beyond Anglican exclusivity. This challenge is important. If it is not taken seriously and made a reality, it will lead to a continued and increased drain away from the state education system of the children of Christian, particularly Evangelical Christian, parents.

Third, the Anglican and the Evangelical share the importance of developing a *theological* rationale for social ethics. Engagement with society and its needs is neither simply a pragmatic response to human need, nor a shared human moral response without any particular reference point. There is such a moral reference point, indeed, a theological one, namely God. The challenge to the Evangelical is to recognize that the quest for biblical social ethics is a legitimate enterprise locally, nationally and globally. It is also the case that Evangelicals need to be willing to engage in the debate, the theological discussion, to recognize that methodology such as the middle axiom is not of necessity incompatible with biblical and Evangelical witness. Here, as elsewhere, the Evangelical also brings a challenge. The theology of the atonement rarely features in theological debate concerning social ethics. This may be because social ethics and evangelism have become too separated, whereas, at least in theological understanding, they belong in close proximity to each other. The dominance of the incarnation as the primary theological motif in Anglican social theology does need – not to be denied – but challenged, by the insights of the atonement. From both their systematic theology and from their heritage, Anglican Evangelicals can bring significant vision, inspiration and discernment. The result could be very powerful, imaginative and engaging indeed.

In drawing these observations together, there are a few other comments to make, both to Evangelicalism and beyond the tradition. First, Evangelicals must not allow the glorious heritage of social engagement and reform to be lost. That engagement has both historic and contemporary expression. It is not and never has been an add-on to other aspects of Evangelical faith; rather, it belongs at the heart of the Evangelical vision of mission. Social reform for the Evangelical is not to be separated from evangelism; they are not the same, but they are related, and the Evangelical vision is to hold them creatively together. Similarly, and importantly, the Evangelical cannot separate their understanding and approach to social reform from the Bible. As we have seen throughout this book, the Bible is the key source and authority for the Evangelical. Historically, also this has been the case for the Anglican. So Anglican Evangelicals will wish to bring the Bible to bear, not only upon the social questions of the day, but also critically in any search for a theological social ethic. The biblical quest lies at the heart of the Anglican Evangelical response to social ethics.

Second, an Anglican Evangelical understanding of social reform will seek to bring to bear the insights of the whole breadth of the tradition. Those most influenced by the Holiness/Pentecostal/charismatic strand of Evangelical opinion have sometimes demonstrated themselves to be the most committed to social welfare at least in the contemporary Church, although the practice has not always flowed from theological conviction (rather, the practice has been driven by need). It is imperative that Reformed Evangelicalism also brings to bear its biblical and theological heritage upon the question. In the past, it was a combination of these theological understandings that gave the movement its power; social reform was not separated from either evangelism or Protestantism generally; the Holiness strand of the tradition, too, brought theological insight. Serious biblical, historic and Evangelical work remains to be done in the theological arena and the debate of ideas.

Third, it is important to note, both for and beyond the Evangelical tradition, that social reform does not just belong to the Evangelical Left or to the political Left. There is a long, if minority, tradition of radical Evangelicalism that has expressed its social theology in both political terms and political praxis. This has been true in both the United States and in England. Indeed, in English terms there has often been a controlling understanding that Evangelical social reform means embracing the political position of the Left. This has been, and remains, immensely damaging to the wider understanding of the Evangelical commitment to social reform. The Evangelical heritage has never occupied this position. If anything, the heritage has been much more to the centre-Right of the political spectrum, embracing a dynamic vision of government responsibility, free market and voluntary agency working in partnership. The Evangelical emphasis on human sin means that the Evangelical Christian will always take a limited view of what can be achieved by simple reliance upon either market forces or government action. The creative imagination comes in the working partnership and with the voluntary sector.

Fourth, then: how are Anglicans Evangelicals to contribute towards recapturing the imagination of the culture in this area of Christian witness? Let me offer some suggestions in addition to what has been written so far. First, the importance of ideas in the public arena, the market square, arguing for the distinctively Christian contribution to society. Evangelicals, alone and with others, need to engage in the public debate to offer a distinctively Christian vision for human society. This is a time for looking outwards, not inwards, to connecting with dissatisfaction with much of what other worldviews offer and with the spiritual longing that has been so often identified. Second, arguing in the Church for the importance of the social agenda. Again, Evangelicals must not leave this agenda as the sole preserve of others – the contribution of Evangelicals to the whole must be genuine, engaging, serious and demonstrably consistent with the theology and history of the movement. Third, in maintaining Evangelical distinctiveness: Evangelicals, not least in conversation with other traditions, need not shy away from maintaining not just Christian distinctiveness, but Evangelical distinctiveness. There are emphases, the authority of the Bible, the importance of the atonement, the priority of transformation and so forth that the Evangelical will wish to ensure remain firmly at the centre of the discussion. Fourth, in creative praxis, Evangelicals will want to demonstrate both the breadth and the nature of their contemporary engagement with society and its social needs as well as its historical commitment. Thus Evangelicals will have expectation that this work will form part of the outreach of an Evangelical church community. Similarly, they will encourage those in urban areas to work at creative approaches to such engagement. From the environment to global warming, from employment to asylum, from homelessness to debt, Evangelicals will want to show the care and love that flows from their theological convictions. The offer of new life has both spiritual and temporal aspects, real meaning needs to be given to being a new creation in Christ. This may involve working with a range of agencies, experimenting with new forms and expressions of church life and finding new and imaginative methods of communication. In all of this, the gospel message, and the need for personal conversion, will remain central.

Notes

1   C. E. Osborne (1903), *Life of Father Dolling*, London, Edward Arnold, quoting Robert Dolling.
2   E. R. Norman (1976), *Church and Society in England 1770–1970*, Oxford, Clarendon Press, chapter 10.
3   The base information has been obtained from the Church of England Education Division.
4   Statement at the first meeting of the National Society, 16 October 1811.
5   The Report of the Commission on Urban Life and Faith (2006), *Faithful Cities*, London, Church House Publishing/Methodist Publishing House.
6   A. Suggate (1987), *William Temple and Christian Social Ethics Today*, Edinburgh, T&T Clark, p. 126.
7   Ibid., p. 127.
8   Ibid., p. 128.
9   *Faithful Cities*, op. cit., p. iv.
10   Ibid., p. v.
11   Ibid., p. 2.
12   Ibid., p. 66.
13   Ibid., p. 67.
14   K. Heasman (1962), *Evangelicals in Action*, London, Geoffrey Bles, p. 14.
15   E. Hodder (1887), *The Life and Work of the Seventh Earl of Shaftesbury*, London, Cassells, vol. ii, p. 3.
16   J. Wolffe (1991), *The Protestant Crusade in Great Britain 1829–1860*, Oxford, Clarendon Press.
17   Lord Ashley, *Proceedings of the Thirteenth Annual Meeting of the London City Mission*, 4 May 1848.
18   Earl of Shaftesbury, Introduction to J. M. Weylland, (1884) *These Fifty Years*, London, S. W. Partridge & Co.
19   Lord Ashley, *Proceedings of the Thirteenth Annual Meeting of the London City Mission*, 4 May 1848.
20   Lord Ashley, *Hansard*, 4 August 1840.
21   Earl of Shaftesbury, Bible Society, *Annual Meeting*, 1851.
22   Earl of Shaftesbury, *Proceedings of the Twenty-eighth Annual Meeting of the London City Mission*, June 1863.
23   Lord Ashley, CPAS, *Abstract*, 1850.
24   Earl of Shaftesbury, CPAS, *Abstract*, 1873.
25   Earl of Shaftesbury, Annual Prize Giving, *RSU Magazine*, vol. 19, April 1967.
26   Earl of Shaftesbury, CPAS, *Abstract*, 1876.
27   T. Chester (1993), *Awakening to a World of Need*, IVP, Leicester, IVP, p. 77.
28   R. D. Williams, The Richard Dimbleby Lecture, 2002.
29   Ibid.
30   Ibid.

Conclusion

The historian of Christianity is ever conscious of the errors and failings of those who over the centuries have claimed to follow Jesus Christ, and the same is true for the historian of Anglicanism and of Evangelicalism. This makes for the need of careful and measured judgements. Historians are also conscious of patterns and of continuities and discontinuities between and within them, for foundation stones and building blocks are also important. The historian will be anxious when themes are detached from their roots. Anglicanism is itself a theme that embraces several others in their own right. The historian of Anglicanism cannot fail to recognize the multifarious ways in which the tradition has developed. All such developments may have some validity, but they are not of equal validity. The historian will look for the links and continuities with the core tradition, the foundation documents and the patterns of thought and ideas.

What then can be said about Anglicanism? First, it is rooted in the Reformation. It is not possible to understand Anglicanism apart from the Reformation. Second, it is grounded in the Bible as its authority in all matters of life and faith. Third, the distinctiveness of the English Reformation was to produce a Reformed episcopal tradition. Fourth, various streams of development took place and were given different weight in various times. Fifth, some of these developments sit in significant ways in discontinuity with historic Anglicanism.

What conclusions can be drawn about Evangelicalism? First, that it too is grounded in the Reformation, but also has been influenced by the more Pietist and Holiness traditions. Second, that it possesses key spiritual marks in the areas of authority (the Bible), doctrine (the substitutionary atonement), spirituality (the personal relationship with Jesus) and transformation (evangelism). Third, that the Evangelical tradition is a spectrum, with differing weight attached to various antecedents explaining either more Reformed or more Charismatic emphasis.

So can these two traditions agree? Or talk to each other? Crucial to understanding this is the recognition that in Anglican Evangelicalism there is already a coherent basis and dialogue which has taken place. There are significant commonalities, especially when the veil is drawn back from the Reformed episcopal heritage of Anglicanism. Sometimes the methodologies are different and there is much that can be learnt, one from another. Even in areas where it might be seen there would be significant differences, such as the transforming impact of the gospel on society, it has been shown that the Evangelical heritage of social concern provides a strong base. The challenge to Anglican Evangelicals is to come to appreciate their heritage so that they carry more conviction and weight as to why they are Anglican as well as Evangelical. The challenge to other Anglican traditions is to recognize that the historic Anglican position sits more at ease with the Anglican Evangelical than it does with many other more recent expressions of the Anglican tradition. Some will find that unpalatable. A greater understanding of the various traditions that go to make up both Evangelicalism and Anglicanism would help to explain not just the areas of common conviction but also why tensions arise. Evangelicals within the Anglican tradition have developed understandings of authority and of ministry that draw directly from the Reformed heritage of Anglicanism; these, however, sit somewhat uneasily with the dominant modern expression of Anglicanism. Can these tensions, whether they be concerned with church planting or sexuality, be resolved? Understanding why they arise is at least a starting point and recognizing the authenticity of the Evangelical position will contribute. Awareness of the ways in which Anglicanism has developed will encourage dialogue. Ultimately there may be sticking points. What is authentically Anglican does not mean the unthinking adoption of every claim of every strand of Anglican history or development. The Evangelical will always want to take the tradition back to its roots. The genuine Evangelical, aware of their own failings and weaknesses, will, however, wish to make and to learn from the links that there are. The Evangelical will always be most anxious when the authority of Scripture is set aside and also when church order is seen to predominate over evangelism.

Evangelicals and Anglicans: can they agree? Yes and no. Yes, in some very significant ways, some surprising, which, as Christians, we are called to build upon. Most especially so because of the historic unity of their shared convictions represented in Anglican Evangelicalism. No, in the sense, that some of the trends within Anglicanism seem to sit at such discontinuity to its historic, biblical expression, that Evangelicals are left with no option but to maintain and proclaim their distinctiveness. However, we are left with a clearer picture of both Anglican and Evangelical traditions and, hopefully, a fuller appreciation of Anglican Evangelicalism.

Bibliography

Avis, P. (2000), *The Anglican Understanding of the Church*, London, SPCK.

Balleine, G. R. (1909), *A History of the Evangelical Party in the Church of England*, London, Longmans.

Bebbington, D. W. (1989), *Evangelicalism in Modern Britain*, London, Unwin Hyman.

Bebbington, D. W. (2005), *The Dominance of Evangelicalism*, Leicester, IVP.

Beckwith, R. (2003), *Elders in Every City*, Carlisle, Paternoster.

Bede, *A History of the English Church and People* (1955), London, Penguin Classics.

Bicknell, E. J. (1955), *A Theological Introduction to the Thirty-Nine Articles of the Church of England*, London, Longmans.

Bradshaw, T. (1992), *The Olive Branch*, Oxford/London, Latimer House/Paternoster.

Brierley, P. (2000), *The Tide is Running Out*, London, Christian Research Association.

Buchanan, C. O. (1998), *Is the Church of England Biblical?*, London, Darton Longman & Todd.

Buchanan, C. O. (1993), *Infant Baptism and the Gospel*, London, Darton Longman & Todd.

Calvin, J. *Institutes of the Christian Religion*, McNeill, J. T. (ed.) Library of Christian Classics, Philadelphia, The Westminster Press.

Chalke, S. and Mann, A. (2003), *The Lost Message of Jesus*, Grand Rapids, Zondervan.

Chester, T. (1993), *Awakening to a World of Need*, Leicester, IVP.

Church of England (1997), *Eucharistic Presidency: a theological statement by the House of Bishops of the General Synod*, London, CHP.

Church of England (2006), The Report of the Commission on Urban Life and Faith, *Faithful Cities*, London, CHP/Methodist Publishing House.

Clark, J. C. D. (2000), *English Society 1688–1832*, 2nd edition, Cambridge, CUP.

Edwards, D. L. (1989), *Christian England*, London, Collins.

Edwards, D. L. and Stott, J. R. W. (1988), *Essentials*, London, Hodder & Stoughton.

Evans, G. R. (2005), *John Wyclif*, Oxford, Lion.

Foxe, J. (1563), *Acts and Monuments of the Christian Church*, edition 1843–49, London.

France, R. T. and McGrath, A. E. (eds) (1993), *Evangelical Anglicans*, London, SPCK.

General Synod of the Church of England, *Report of Proceedings*, London, CHP.

Green, C. (ed.) (2006), *Guarding the Gospel*, Grand Rapids, Zondervan.

Heasman, K. (1962), *Evangelicals in Action*, London, Geoffrey Bles.

Jackson, R. (2002), *Hope for the Church*, London, CHP.

Jackson, R. (2005), *The Road to Growth*, London, CHP.

Jewell, J., *An Apology of the Church of England*, Booty, J. (ed.) (1963), New York, Cornell.

Hodder, E. (1892), *The Life and Work of the Seventh Earl of Shaftesbury K. G.*, London, Cassells.

Hodder, E. (1887), *The Life and Work of the Seventh Earl of Shaftesbury*, 3 vols, London, Cassells.

Lewis, D. (1986), *Lighten their Darkness*, New York, Greenwood Press.

MacCulloch, D. (1996), *Thomas Cranmer*, New York and London, Yale.

McGrath, A. E. (1994), *Evangelicalism and the Future of Christianity*, London, Hodder & Stoughton.

Morris, L. (1955), *The Apostolic Preaching of the Cross*, London, Tyndale Press.

Myers, A. R. (ed.) (1969), *English Historical Documents, AD 327–1485*.

Nicholson, The Revd W. R. (1875), *Reasons Why I Became A Reformed Episcopalian*, Philadelphia.

Noll, M. A. (2004), *The Rise of Evangelicalism*, Leicester, Apollos.

Noll, M. A., Bebbington, D. W. and Rawlyk, G. A. (1994), *Evangelicalism*, New York, OUP.

Norman, E. R. (1976), *Church and Society in England 1770–1970*, Oxford, Clarendon Press.

Osborne, C. E. (1903), *Life of Father Dolling*, London, Edward Arnold.

Packer, J. I. (1978), *The Evangelical Anglican Identity Problem*, Oxford, Latimer Studies 1, Latimer House.

Patten, S. (ed.) (2003), *Anglicanism and the Western Christian Tradition*, Norwich, Canterbury Press.

Podmore, C. (2005), *Aspects of Anglican Identity*, London, CHP.

Pratt. J. H. (ed.) (1865), *The Thought of the Evangelical Leaders: notes of the discussions of The Eclectic Society, London during the years 1798–1814*, reprinted 1978, Edinburgh, Banner of Truth.

Seitz, C. R. (2001), *Figured Out*, Louisville, John Knox Press.

Stott, J. R. W. (1986), *The Cross of Christ*, Leicester, IVP.

Suggate, A. (1987), *William Temple and Christian Social Ethics Today*, Edinburgh, T&T Clark.

Sykes, S. and Booty, J. (eds) (1988), *The Study of Anglicanism*, London, SPCK.

Toon, P. (1979), *Evangelical Theology 1833–1856*, London, Marshall, Morgan and Scott.

Turnbull, R. D. (1993), 'The emergence of the Protestant Evangelical tradition', *Churchman*, vol. 107, no. 4.

Turnbull, R. D. (1997), *The place of the 7th Earl of Shaftesbury within the Evangelical tradition, with particular reference to his understanding of the relationship of evangelistic mission to social reform*, Durham, University of Durham Ph.D. thesis.

Turnbull, R. D. (1999), 'Evangelicalism: the state of scholarship and the question of identity', *Anvil*, vol. 16, no. 2.

Walsh, J. D. (1966), 'Origins of the Evangelical Revival', in Bennett, G. V. and Walsh, J. D., *Essays in Modern English Church History*, New York, OUP.

Wesley, J., *Journal*. Standard edition, 1909–16, London, Epworth Press.

Williams, R. (2004), *Anglican Identities*, London, Darton Longman & Todd.

Wolffe, J. (1991), *The Protestant Crusade in Great Britain 1829–1860*, Oxford, Clarendon Press.

Zahl, P. F. M. (1998), *The Protestant Face of Anglicanism*, Grand Rapids, Eerdmans.

Index of names and subjects